Life's Source Code

Life's Source Code
Unlocking the Secrets to Transform Your Life and Realize Your Dreams

Gary K. Yamamoto

Cypress Mountain Books
An Imprint of Dynamic Pathways, Inc.
Tucson, AZ

LIFE'S SOURCE CODE
Copyright © 2022 Gary K. Yamamoto
Cover photo by Trace Hudson

Library of Congress Control Number: 2022917732

ISBN: 9781878182104 (eBook)
ISBN: 9781878182111 (paperback)

Contents

Dedication

Andrea Gold: *My wonderful wife who continues to support me and keep me focused on my passion and mission. She never lost faith in what we will accomplish.*

Masaru and Kikue Yamamoto: *My parents sacrificed so much and provided me with the opportunities I needed.*

Frank Candy: *A true friend and fellow speakers bureau owner. His insights and edits have immensely helped to improve this book.*

Achim and Jane Ihlenfeld: *True supporters who have given me helpful advice. They also reviewed and guided this book.*

Jane Ihlenfeld and Ethel Tom: *My sisters who put up with me while growing up and who taught me what it's like to love and be real supporters.*

Bill and Valerie Southwood: *They were my powerful mentors and the most wonderful teachers and supporters.*

Patricia Diegel: *A brilliant teacher who said, "You're to teach Eastern knowledge with Western practical approaches."*

Bill Dutcher: *Bill shared the keys to the Hawaiian practice of Kahuna.*

Hawayo Takata: *She verified I had the healing ability before I was initiated by her.*

Jon Diegel: *He was my brilliant teacher of spirituality, religion, and presentations.*

Macelle Brown: *Astrologer who motivated me to transform my life by saying, "The rest of your life will be wonderful."*

Forrest Wellington: *He was an amazing doctor and healer who worked on me and taught me more methods of healing.*

Gail Minogue: *She said writing is my destiny and urged me to continue writing.*

Readers of this book: *I also dedicate this book to all who are on their journey up the mountain of life. I wish you much success on your journey and celebrate your success.*

This book will open the door to possibilities or confirm your experiences during a lifetime of adventure and exploration!

Preface

Answering your questions, "Who am I? Why am I here? Where am I going? How will I get there? Who or what will help me? Is there a purpose for my life?"

For thousands of years, humans have been trying to answer the above questions. The few who found answers came through a very long and arduous route. It took them many lifetimes of training and sacrifice.

Today, we live in a different age. Through millions of years of evolution, we have become the top dogs on the planet. We are the only creatures to be able to think with intelligence. We are peering into the level of mind that can't be physically measured. To delve into the above questions, we must make a quantum leap into a different level of awareness. We can choose to do this because it promises to free us from suffering into a life of adventure, challenges, love, joy, and/or peace of mind.

Not wanting to follow the usual corridors of life, I've spent the past 70 years in search of different pathways and a new way of living. My journey took me into the martial art of Aikido, Buddhism, electrical engineering, metaphysics, ordination as a Catholic Priest, business owner, and professional speaking.

My purpose for writing this book is to give you what I've gained over my lifetime. By taking the best I've experienced and learned, you can avoid starting from ground zero. Then, by transforming your life, my wish for you is to go on, spread the word, and create a world that's better than what I envision. While my promises may seem wonderful, the work may be long and hard.

Each chapter provides you with methods to improve your life. These methods are easy to learn and simple enough to apply. But that's never enough. It's the constant application that allows you to truly live the knowledge and empower yourself. In time, you too will be able to share the wisdom found in your new way of living. You'll find that life is more than the acquisition and hoarding of things. You'll know how precious love, joy, and peace of mind are, and how quickly they can be lost. You'll understand how life is to discover possibilities, enjoy what you've created, and learn from mistakes.

You are a powerful person, able to choose however you wish to live. If you don't like where you're going, only you can change it. When you establish your purpose, the life-forces will help you to succeed. Life then becomes a continuous and unfolding adventure.

Introduction

You're here at the best time in history to transform your life. You'll start by understanding how the Source operates. I'm using the word "Source" instead of Creator or God. The latter words have a lot of emotional beliefs attached to them. When we discuss the Source, you won't have limitations or beliefs interfering with what you're reading.

With this understanding, you'll gain control of your life. You'll know why some things work for you and others drag you down. But control is a double-edged sword. It also means that you're responsible for all your choices and actions. So, whether your life is great or sucks, you're responsible for the results you receive.

This book gives you a new roadmap for life. You'll learn the existence of life-forces and how they influence what happens in your future. You'll get answers to your critical questions, such as:

- Why are some people geniuses?
- Why so few are very rich?
- Why so many are poor and suffering?
- What are the forces that influence your life?

This book is my attempt to present a new and simple approach to life. You'll be able to transform your life and create the life of your dreams. But this message is not new. When the world first started moving into the Next Age, new knowledge and peace opened the hearts and minds of only a few. The purveyors of drugs easily corrupted them. When this movement failed to interest the masses, the powerful motivator of pain then spread across the land. Will it take hell on Earth before people stop the old ways and embrace the new?

When the new emerges, the quiet ones have seen the signs of the times and have prepared. They'll flow with the ending of the old and transform themselves. The late adopters may scorn and ridicule the early ones. In time, they'll eventually stop resisting, understand, and finally accept the new.

You'll see that while happiness is fleeting, joy is always available from within. Sex and relationships come and go, while love is eternal. And while safety and security appear to have some permanence, only peace of mind is everlasting. Love, joy, and peace of mind are not states you need to chase after; they are your birthright to experience and enjoy right now.

The important question for you is, "Are you willing to transform your life, or will you wait to be dragged, kicking and screaming, into the new?" You have a simple question waiting for a positive answer. "Are you ready?"

What is Life?

Life is either a great adventure or nothing.
— Helen Keller

There are moments in your life that made you realize there was more going on than you realized. When these expectedly occurred, you probably called them lucky breaks or the unique alignment of the stars. When this happened to my wife and me, the full extent of this story didn't become apparent until the following week. This one occurred after having our usual Saturday morning breakfast at a restaurant in Tucson, Arizona.

After breakfast, my wife and I got into our car to head to our office. I always took the exit that would take us north and turned west to our office. As I drove towards the usual exit to head north, I drove around the restaurant to another exit. I got into the lane that went west and waited at the light. My wife said I could still get into the right turn lane and head north, but I just ignored her. As we drove west, she asked why I was going this way. I replied, "I don't know."

Shortly after arriving at our office, we heard emergency vehicles. Although emergency vehicles to and from the hospital were common, more sirens kept sounding off. Later, my wife received a frantic call from her mother. She was crying and frantically asking if we were alright.

We had planned to meet her that morning at Gabby Gifford's Congress on the Corner. She was afraid we were there during the shooting. Somehow, we had forgotten our plans to meet her there. She was not there on time because a phone call had delayed her. She arrived to find the streets closed off and thought we were there.

The next week that realized the significance of changing my usual driving route at the same restaurant. When the server recognized us, she asked if we recalled the person who checked out just before us. My wife remembered he was an older man. The server said he was the one who attended the Gabby Gifford meeting and was killed protecting his wife. We realized that if we had headed north, we would have been a minute behind him. When we got close to where the meeting was being held, we would have remembered we were going there. We would have been in the middle of the shooting.

This incident made me realize that something very significant had happened here. I initially thought I had a dream that had warned me. I've come to realize that my course change to the office may have been the work of my life-forces. I'll explain the life-forces later in this book.

Life is a Journey

You're on a journey, an adventure through life. You're here to transform your life, much as a caterpillar becomes a beautiful butterfly. When you witnessed miracles, you thought there must be more to life than you've known. You've heard about those who have returned from clinical death and shared so many wonderful stories. In your heart, you could sense that there are angels, guardians, guides, and devas. These life-forces are helping you to rise above your present situation. You may have even glimpsed their presence during your quiet moments and dreams.

You quietly want to leave behind your present life based on the old beliefs of science, religion, and government. In its place, you want a new vision to drive your life; one based on individual "knowledge and freedom." This will be driven by new ideas you're hoping to uncover through personal experience. Unfortunately, you found yourself trapped within the limiting mindset of society. When you went on your unique pathway, people may have criticized, ridiculed, and even hated you. The prevailing standards and beliefs of society repeatedly pushed you back and even dragged you down. Let's see how these systems limited possibilities.

Life According to Science

Science taught how you're the evolutionary product of meteors and comets striking the Earth. Over many billions of years, these rocks brought with them water that held the building blocks of life. From that, all the life forms on this planet evolved. Like all life forms, your driving purpose was to survive and procreate. What you can see and measure is all there is. When you die, science says it's over! Nothing of you survives. End of story! Yet you may have had dreams and visitations from family members who have passed over. But science says it's all in your mind. You intuitively felt there's more to life than one round and done. Are you ready to explore possibilities?

Life According to Western Religion

Here you learned how God created the universe in six days and rested for a day. The first humans broke the only law God gave them and ate from the tree of the knowledge of good and evil. That taught them right from wrong. For that, God threw them out of the garden and life became hard work. You learned you had only one chance to live a righteous life or suffer an eternity in hell. You prayed for salvation and practiced your rituals and ceremonies. All the while, the saints and mystics have shared a different message. Their messages and miracles opened the minds and hearts of those who were ready. Have you heard and felt their messages?

Life According to Eastern Religion

The origin of life on the planet is not a primary concern of these religions. They say your life is just the product of what you did in your past lives. Your bad karma will give you many lifetimes of pain and suffering. By doing good, you'll release negative karma until you achieve enlightenment. Enlightenment will liberate you from the endless cycle of birth and death, but that is almost impossible to achieve. If you wish to achieve enlightenment, you'll do your expected meditation, prayers, rituals, ceremonies, and good deeds to gain good karma. Eventually, you hope to achieve enlightenment. Are you making much progress?

Life According to Government

If you don't believe in science or religion, then the ruling monarchy or government becomes your god. They create the laws, rules, and regulations you must follow. Break these and they will fine, incarcerate, beat, and/or execute you. Leaders enjoy tremendous privileges and standards of living relative to the masses. Some control through force, backed by police and the military. Others control through Robin Hood tactics, taking from the rich and giving to the poor. Unless you're one of the privileged few, your life becomes one of servitude and asking for jobs or handouts. Are you wondering if this is all there is to life?

Life According to the Author

You're a child of the Source, an independent spirit. The essence of you was at the very beginning and will be until the end. You have access to the Source's knowledge and power.

You're here to experience the possibilities life on Earth offers. At all times, you can transform your life and change the world around you. You'll discover your own truths based on your best experiences and realizations.

I'm not saying you should stop believing what science, religion, or government says. I'm suggesting you move beyond their limitations. Life offers a universe of possibilities, open to anyone who searches for them. Are you flexible and strong enough to look at life differently, take new actions, and rise above your present limited life?

Summary

This is a new way of living that provides you with freedom and control. To get there, I've spent 70+ years of my life searching and experiencing what's possible. I'm sharing what I've gathered from my background in science, metaphysics, religion, business, author, and spirituality.

Letting go gives you freedom.

The Search for Answers

*Your best knowledge and actions created what you
have.
If you don't like it, release the old to discover the
new!*

L et's start here with a summary of what made me think I was an authority on the Source. Deep inside, I was driven by the need to help people. I knew that life was more than having a good job, raising a family, and then retiring comfortably. So, I ventured down a lesser-traveled path, into the spiritual and metaphysical. I was looking for answers, real answers. Over the past 70 years, I studied, struggled, found, proved, and lived it. Now, I want to give it to you. To do this, you're invited to join me on a journey. You'll transform your life and get the most out of every single day.

For me, it started with a single incident that would change the course of my life. Sitting in the front pew at the funeral of my paternal grandmother, I heard a strange voice asking,

"Why do people have to die?"

Glancing up and down the pew, there was no one except my parents and sisters. After a couple of minutes, I heard the same message. I mentally repeated the phrase to remember it. When the Buddhist priest began chanting, the voice stopped. The sound of the chanting somehow felt comforting. When the priest hit the gong, it sounded strangely familiar. I didn't know why, but I enjoyed hearing it. From that time, I would occasionally wonder why people had to die.

*In this world, everyone must die. None of us has any
choice in that. Our choice is how we wish to live. —*
Terry Goodkind

Aikido

It was at the funeral that my uncle, Sadao Yoshioka, told my
parents I should enroll in Aikido. My parents quickly agreed and
took me down to buy a cool martial arts outfit. I began training
the next Saturday. At the end of each training session, we
meditated to the count of the instructor. The instructor always
closed by telling us to practice meditation at home. As I'm
writing this book, I've been meditating for the past 70 years.

It took me over 20 years of daily meditation to achieve a silent
mind. Later in this book, you'll learn a simple meditation
method. You'll be able to cut the time to achieve a silent mind.
When you do, you'll be living a life with much less stress and
misery.

Aikido cannot be anything but a martial art of love.
— Morihei Ueshiba, Founder of Aikido

Buddhism

Early in my life, I considered becoming a Buddhist priest,
although I coveted becoming an engineer. Perhaps this religion
could provide the answers to questions about life. Attending
memorial services for my grandmother inspired me to immerse
myself in an extensive, year-long course in Buddhism. The
timing was just right; I was ready to learn the principles of
Buddhism and explore other Eastern religions.

While studying Buddhism appears to be complicated, the
basic principles are powerful. For instance, Buddhist prayer is
not asking for help or assistance. It assumes that the Source loves
you and is doing what it can to help you. A Buddhist prays to
simply thank Buddha (the Source) for everything he has and
continues to provide.

Buddhist prayer is to give thanks for all that has been and will be given to you.

Engineering Mindset

After graduating with a degree in electrical engineering, I quickly found interesting work in several fields. My education and work enabled me to see most things as a process of how things worked, including life. I realized the profundity and power in the concept that all of life is nothing more than energy. It enabled me to simplify complex processes into simple methods to transform people's lives. I've organized and simplified this book into processes.

A friend once asked me how I could so easily switch from religion to engineering. My quick answer was simple:

Religion deals with a powerful force and if you screw up, you can get hurt. Electrical engineering deals with a powerful energy and if you screw up, you will get hurt.

Metaphysics Mindset

In the summer of 1972, a metaphysical bookstore opened in Honolulu. The instructors were teaching a wide variety of topics. I discovered there was more to life than what I knew or understood. I was guided to take different classes that I was open to learning, using, and improving.

Yesterday I was clever, so I wanted to change the world. Today I am wise, so I am changing myself.
— Rumi

The Source guided me to the best books written by mystics and saints who described their experiences. When I taught classes, I found them fulfilling, and they intensified my learning. I enjoyed living a dual life, an engineer during the day and a metaphysician in the evening and on weekends.

Leaving Paradise

Several years later, my former wife and I moved to Arizona. She wanted to live in Sedona and my job was 300 miles away. I would commute on weekends to go home and usually teach classes in Sedona.

Catholic Priest

Still interested in religion, I took my seminary training in Phoenix, Arizona. Archbishop Patriarch Adrian Spruit ordained me as a priest in the Malabar Rites of the Catholic Church. It's often called the Liberal Catholic Church because it allows priests to be married and women to be priests. It gave me a deeper understanding of the Christian religion and what Christians believed.

> *...for the one who is in you is greater than the one who is in this world.* — Jesus

Divorce

Except for the 300-mile drive between my work and home in Sedona, my smooth and easygoing Hawaiian way of living continued. But as they always say,

> *When everything seems to be going well, you have obviously overlooked something.* — Steven Wright

I discovered what I had overlooked when my wife sued for divorce. The ex-wife took all the money from the Hawaii real estate deals. I got the tens of thousands of dollars in credit card debt she had accumulated. They gave me the house with a mortgage in Sedona. Located 300 miles from my job. I struggled to rent the house and finally sold it at a huge loss. The IRS then hit me with my ex's back taxes, penalties, and interest. They claimed I owed the taxes because I was still married to her. I was in no position to fight them.

Self-Discovery

It was at that point that the world stopped for me. I wasn't angry or upset. Having a meditative mind, the ex-wife just disappeared from my life. My life was moving on.

> *You will face many defeats in life, but never let yourself be defeated.* — Maya Angelou

This was my opportunity to discover my own truth about life. I created a personal prayer and meditation retreat. My nearly empty apartment was perfect. I had no furniture except for a comfortable chair and a 4-inch foam mattress to sleep on. I also had a desktop computer. My only interruption would be time at work to continue paying bills.

Deep inside, I believed that this shouldn't take long. After all, Gautama Buddha sat under the Bodhi tree for only 49 days before enlightenment. I had decades more meditation experience than he did. Jesus fought the devil for 40 days in the desert. Already living in the Arizona desert, how difficult could it be to resist any temptation, even if it lasted more than 40 days?

In a short time, I began receiving a lot of answers, insights, realizations, and experiences. The profundity of these became clear as I sat in contemplation. I saw how unseen forces had led my life and had occasionally fed me new thoughts and beliefs. When sharing these new ideas, it astounded me how easily people rejected these. They allowed themselves to be controlled by fear, anger, and hate.

Work was also evolving and changing quickly. The state-of-the-art was quickly moving into satellites, fiber optic cables, and high-speed digital communications. Computers were getting faster with more built-in memory. But what I saw was more of the same thing, with faster and smaller equipment. My work had become monotonous!

Let what comes come. Let what goes go. Find out what remains. — Ramana Maharshi

You'll learn how to use this book to transform your life and change your world. It was these principles that led me into the next stages of my life. By understanding the principles of the Source Code, you will quickly start to transform your life.

Publishing

I had a dream to publish my book on dream interpretation. Unfortunately, back in the early 1980s, it was nearly impossible to get a publisher interested in it. That left only one avenue open to me. I seemed to be guided to resign from my US Government job, withdraw all my retirement money, and start a trade book publishing company. I did this with no knowledge of the publishing business. A couple of people at work thought this was either stupid or crazy. But I did it and we named the company Harbinger House because it sounded old and established.

Hiring several publishing experts, we published my dream book, Creative Dream Analysis: A Guide to Personal Development. The company began publishing more books, including two of my children's books. I eventually sold my part of the company to my partner.

Start a Speakers Bureau

As you'll read in the chapter on allowing, my wife, Andrea, and I did not intend to start a speakers bureau. We had no knowledge of speakers bureaus or professional speakers. We were literally led to create and get into the speakers bureau business.

We founded the Gold Stars Speakers Bureau in 1990 and became one of the most respected and influential speakers bureaus in the country. Our clients are good people who work for or represented corporations, trade associations, and government agencies.

Gold Stars Speakers Bureau represents and books well-known and successful authors, athletes, astronauts, subject-matter experts, and celebrities for special events, business meetings, and conventions. They influence the thinking, performance, and productivity of small and huge organizations. It's been a rare privilege and honor for Andrea and me to be a part of this wonderful business and make a big difference in the lives of so many people.

Speaker

Naturally, I had a marketing arm to speak to people. I tailored my messages to meet the attendees' needs, based on two principles: 1) Give people what they want, while also providing them with what they need, and 2) Make sure it's relevant, valuable, and easy to implement.

Your ability to speak coherently is important in your life. It's even more important to listen and understand what others have to say. By being attentive, you'll also hear what they're not saying.

Author

Last year, the Source inspired me to organize and publish this information for people just like you. Until the last decade, traditional publishing was a huge hurdle and controlled by the major publishing houses in New York. However, the disruptive world of self-publishing allows good people like you and me to share our experiences, strengths, and hopes with the world. This is the beginning of many books I'll be releasing to help you through life.

Summary

You have a choice. You can use the traditional methods of personal development that will give you some results. Or you can follow the methods in this book and begin transforming your life to get positive results quickly. You'll take my words, test my ideas and suggestions, and evaluate the results. You'll transform yourself to minimize limitations and suffering. You can then create a life you'll fully enjoy.

In the next section, you'll begin by understanding the Source or Higher Power. The enlightened beings of the past describe the Source as being omnipresent, omnipotent, and omniscient. Are you ready to discover the answer to "Who and what are you?

Code 1: The Source

*When you understand the Source, you understand
who you are and what becomes possible.*

Y ou now know I've been searching for answers for over 70 years. What I've gotten has been a wonderful adventure. My approach has been a combination of science, religion, metaphysics, and business. As an engineer, I'm always looking for practical answers. If it's useful, I'll keep it. If not, I discard it. Religion showed me how many people are searching for answers, answers they can experience and use in their daily lives. Metaphysics gave insights that there was more to life that I needed to discover. And business taught me that unless you're making a return on your investment, you only have a hobby.

Most people who search for answers start with the problems people have. Instead of doing this, I wanted to start at the top. I wanted to know about the top dog of life; I wanted to know the Source. When you know the Source, you'll know who and what you are! The world's greatest mystics and saints have defined the Source as being omnipresent, omnipotent, and omniscient. Let's see what these mean and how you can apply these principles into your life.

Omnipresent

This means the Source is everywhere at all times. The Source is not somewhere else, spying on your life. Instead, the Source is the universe and beyond. When you look at the night sky around you, the Source is all the planets, stars, galaxies, and black holes. It's also the dark matter and energy that remains unseen.

Our entire planet is also a part of the Source. Your body, along with everything you think, feel, and do, flows through the

Source. It's the same for everyone else in the world. This sense of oneness extends throughout the universe.

Once you realize you're a part of the Source, the following insights become clear.

- You're no longer a limited being. You're a part of the most powerful entity in the Universe. This gives you the power and freedom to chart a unique pathway through life.

- While your body will eventually die, the essence or spirit is a part of the Source and will always exist. Have courage because the essence or the real you can never end.

- Everyone in the world is also a part of the Source. Essentially, you have a common bond with everyone else on the planet.

You are nothing less than Source material. You are connected to everyone on the planet. In fact, you're connected with everything in the universe. You can safely say that you and the Source are one.

Omnipotent

Omnipotent means to be all-powerful. It means that there's no other power as powerful or nearly as powerful as the Source. There's no Satan or Devil that can challenge the power of the Source. Everything in the universe owes its total energy and existence to the Source. From your point of view, the power of the Source is unlimited.

The Source provides your life energy. You have a tremendous potential to create whatever you wish. Stop for a moment and look around. What you see is what you believe is possible in your life. As you transform your life, you (and the world around you) will adapt to reflect your new beliefs. Are you ready to exercise some of your inherent power?

Omniscient

An Omniscient Source is all-knowing. It knows everything that has happened from the beginning of this creation cycle till now. It knows the multiple dimensions and existences beyond what you can even imagine. While your brain can't comprehend even the tiniest sliver of the total knowledge of the universe, it has access to parts of it. You'll realize that the Source even knows your probable future. While forces are supporting the life you chose, your free will allows you to make any changes you desire. Are you ready to make a meaningful change?

Summary

The essence of you is an immortal being. Your essence took on a physical body for this lifetime of experiences. This body allows you to experience pleasure, but it also feels pain. With a body, you are free to create, play, and enjoy all the wonderful possibilities that are available. But if you abuse it, you will suffer the results. Through a lifetime of use and hard use, your body becomes worn out, ill, or badly damaged. At some point, your essence will choose to release that body. Your essence can then choose to hang around to help loved ones or get ready for the next incarnation into this world. The Source has given you the most precious gift—life.

You and the Source are one!

Code 2: Our Prime Directives

Life is really simple, but we insist on making it complicated. — Confucius

You now know who and what you are. Your next question is probably to ask if there is something that you should do. Does the Source have a plan or outline of something that it wants you to accomplish in a lifetime? And if there is a plan, is it specifically aimed at you? In other words, has the Source assigned a personal mission that you need to accomplish during your lifetime?

Like everyone else, the Source didn't assign you a specific mission or plan you needed to follow. What you had was a general set of directives that applied to everyone. At a young age, you decided what you want to do with your life. At any point in your life, you had the freedom to make a change and go in a different direction. You still have that option right now!

It's impossible to completely understand the Source. Through research, meditative insights, and realizations, I've gathered the following that applies to humanity. This is a simple set of instructions that reveals your general purpose for a lifetime on Earth. You have the freedom to interpret and use these in any way you see fit.

The 3 Prime Directives

These are our prime directives on how to live your life:

- Discover what is possible.
- Enjoy your life.
- Learn from what you have created.

Humanity has made significant technological progress during the past century. It's difficult to fathom how much further people can evolve physically and psychologically. Let's see how you can also transform your personal life.

Discover What's Possible

You live in a vast and unlimited universe. When you were born, you had an urge to discover new and different things. From childhood, your inquisitive mind sought to increase your skills and knowledge. It wanted to understand how things were and then see what else was possible. By maintaining an open mind, what you can observe, learn, and discover may astound you!

You're living in a world where there are so many physical and psychological problems. People are suffering from so many forms of pain and suffering. The world is open to you to expand your skills and knowledge to discover new and unique solutions. This is the challenge you and everyone else in the world faces.

Enjoy Life

Are you enjoying your life? You may quickly say "yes." But does your enjoyment only come when you take part in something good? If you played a terrible round of golf, was it enjoyable? If a planned romantic evening with a partner became embarrassing, did you enjoy it? Yet, it's possible to enjoy even the simplest moments of your life.

For instance, can you observe the same scene view every morning and still find it beautiful? It happened to me as I sat on the front steps of my home in Hawaii.

> *Every morning, I sat on the stairs, tying my shoelaces before going to work. For more than a year, I looked up at the same view of Pearl Harbor. I enjoyed that stunning view as if I was looking at it for the first time. My secret was being silent and aware of my surroundings.*

As a boy scout hiking the Kalalau Trail on the Island of Kauai in Hawaii, I got my first hint of the secret to enjoying life.

It was one of those hot summer days when we began hiking along the Na Pali Coast. I was a young boy scout who joined the troop two weeks earlier. It was a tough 22-mile hike. We would hike in on the first day and hike back out the following day.

Hiking up and down, in and out of the valleys on a narrow trail was hot, humid, and tiring. I was lagging in the back, thinking this was a miserable way to spend my summer vacation. After a couple of hours of hiking, the heat was really getting to me. My shoulders were aching as my backpack kept getting heavier. Desperation made me pray it would get cooler. My prayers were soon answered with what I would describe as a downpour. The trail became slippery with mud and scary as one side of the trail slipped off the edge of a cliff. The rain eventually lessened to a constant drizzle.

At the end of the trail, we pitched our Army pup tents on the wet ground. For dinner, we had planned to have a warm meal of corned beef and cabbage. But with nothing but wet wood on the ground, I stared at my plate of greasy corned beef and raw cabbage. My scoutmaster stopped to watch me pour out the rainwater that had collected on my plate. Looking down at me, he asked,

"Gary, are you having fun yet?"

I looked up with my saddest face and dragged out a long, "Noooo..."

He then looked up at the tall mountain cliffs that dropped to the ocean. The evening sky had turned into different shades of orange and crimson. Below, the ocean seemed to reflect the colors of the sky striped with white waves along the shore. He continued looking at the view and said,

"Gary, you should try to have some fun, because life doesn't get much better than this."

I had no idea what my scoutmaster was talking about. I was suffering from one of the worst days of my young life. My scoutmaster wasn't concentrating on the rain or the terrible meal. If he had, he may have also felt miserable. But he placed his focus on the sunset, the explosion of color, and enjoyed the moment. When you have a positive mindset, you can usually enjoy so many more wonderful moments in your life. By focusing on what you have and not what's missing, life becomes enjoyable.

Continuous Learning

Here, you get to experience and learn from your life and the lives of others. In this world, there will always be the poor and suffering. There can be no utopia as long as people are acting stupid or greedy. When you see this, your choice is to either respond with intelligence or react with stupidity. When you see how others are reacting stupidly, you should resolve to never do the same.

Your life is the result of what you created. You may have created a successful company that made you wealthy. While society may worship and praise your accomplishment, what was the complete result of what you created?

What you learned and gained in the physical world may be wonderful, but there's more to life than that. Life is also about how you worked and interacted with people. Even a sole entrepreneur has to interact with suppliers and customers. Everything you accomplished was through the support and help of others. Your best lessons often come from your worst failures.

Did you learn the best way to treat the people who were working with and for you? Did the way other people treated you reveal what to do or not do? Did you get any feedback about your behavior and methods? What will you change to be better the next time? Of course, fair treatment doesn't mean you bend over backward and cater to ridiculous needs and desires.

You're either learning and improving based on your experiences, or you're not. When you don't learn and improve, you invite retribution from your past. You will understand this when you learn more about how the actions of Dharma and karma influence your life.

Summary

You are a powerful being on an adventurous journey. Life is a simple process. You're here to discover whatever you desire. You should enjoy life while learning from your experiences. As the child of the Source, you can turn your life into an exciting adventure or let it become a life filled with misery and suffering. As always, the choice is yours!

Code 3: Dharma

Understanding the invisible yet powerful forces in your life.

W e now get into something that's a little heavy. Dharma is an Eastern Religion term that dictates the order of everything that exists in the universe. Right now, the universe is expanding at the speed of thought, which is faster than the speed of light. Similarly, Dharma wants you to expand what you do and create. It's your inner desire to expand whatever you're doing and discover what else is possible. Dharma impels you to live a life without boundaries. It causes you to do your best at whatever you choose to do. Dharma doesn't care what you expand, only that you do.

The Myth of Equality

Every person who starts or runs a business wants it to be larger. Each salesperson wants to sell more of the products and services the company offers. The Source tends to richly reward anyone who pushes beyond the limits of the norm. That's good from their point of view. Other people look at the increasing wealth of the rich and become jealous. They too want to increase their wealth and have not done very well. That creates conflict. The nature of Dharma is to reward those who increase and limit those who don't.

> *For to all those who have, more will be given, and they will have an abundance; but from those who have nothing, even what they have will be taken away.* — Jesus

In the same way, the best musicians who create the best-loved music are generally the highest-paid. The best-loved art garners the highest incomes. It's the same for the best criminals and con artists. The rewards always go to the best, the hardest working, and the most innovative. There will always be those who are extremely wealthy. Similarly, there will always be many who will be poor. Life is a game where the rewards go to those who create the best and expand what they're doing. They are following the prime directive of discovering what's possible.

Many of the changes have focused on the physical and mental. Individuals have increased their ownership of land and precious collectibles. They have studied to learn in whatever field they chose. What they lack is the drive to know more about their inner lives. For many, a couple of hours visiting their religious organization is seen as sufficient. Others do it through the internet or watch it on their television sets. Still others add regular sessions of yoga and meditation. They may miss the larger scope of what their inner life offers. Imagine a life living with love, joy, and peace of mind.

Inner Growth

Just as you have a desire for physical growth, you have that same desire for inner growth. You have a natural curiosity to discover the true nature of your inner life. You know there's more to life than simply gathering more wealth and the toys of the wealthy.

Today, there are thousands of books and classes that teach you how to become spiritual. They offer classes in meditation or teach you different Yoga poses. Even martial arts are primarily an inner training. As the Aikido founder has said, his training was about love. These are all stepping stones to living a life of love, joy, and peace of mind. But knowledge of the inner is not enough. You're required to actively practice what you've learned over your lifetime.

Behavior

Dharma outlines what you should consider as right and wrong behavior. It considers what you did and all the reasoning and conditions behind your actions. It also looks at any outside influences, your intent, the intent of other people, and so many other subtle factors. These combine to determine the results of what you created. With Dharma, there are no set rules and fixed judgments on what makes the right behavior. It's left to us to simply do the best we can and leave it for Dharma to evaluate and judge.

Free Will

Dharma gives you the ability to choose whatever you wish in life. You can do and say anything you wish. You can have whatever thoughts you wish to have. But along with that, you will take responsibility for your thoughts, words, and actions.

Judge Not

It's best not to judge the actions and beliefs of anyone. For instance, some vegetarians criticize those who believe in killing and consuming animal life forms. However, they see nothing wrong with killing plant life forms to survive. Essentially, we are all killing and eating life forms.

You must kill to eat and survive. Or, you must have someone kill for you. But is it possible to see and live life differently? Can you understand that your meal is a sacrifice of the life forms you consume? Can you express thanks for the sacrifice of the life form that allows you to survive and enjoy life? Hence, the ancients created prayer to thank God (the entities we eat) for nourishing them.

Prayer became a regular practice during meals. You can give thanks to the Source (the life forms) for providing this food (sacrificing their lives) so that you may grow and prosper. It's also a good practice to bless and purify the food and water before you eat and drink. That allows your meal to better nourish and heal you.

By giving thanks, you've lifted yourself above the behavior of the lower animals. Essentially, you realize that life is more than survival and procreation. While some people may choose to act and live as human animals, that isn't your true nature. You've evolved to a higher level of consciousness and intelligence.

You cannot truly judge what you and anyone else are doing. Only Dharma sees the total result of everything a person does. You can never see the totality of the action and the results it created. You must leave the final judgment to Dharma.

Problems

Being spiritual doesn't mean you won't have problems. In fact, as you expand your life, larger problems will confront you. Can you see bigger problems as an indication that you're growing and evolving? There may be more demand for your time and expertise. You may be required to act in a certain way to fulfill your role or position. And solving one problem often creates other problems. This is the nature of life. As Mark Twain once wrote, "Life is just one damn thing after another."

As a speaker, I've asked attendees to raise their hands if they liked having problems at work. There's rarely a time when someone raises their hand. I explain that the only reason you're working and being paid was because your company had problems. Your boss hired you to solve those problems. Your manager didn't want you to complain or ask her to solve your work problems. She expected you to provide quick solutions. So, when you return to work, be happy to find problems waiting for you. If there were no problems, the company may no longer need you.

Summary

Dharma wants you to expand your life and succeed. That's it!

Code 4: The Allowing Lifestyle

Life is a miracle. Everything else is a bonus.

I've mentioned the existence of life-forces before. Life-forces include Dharma, guardians, angels, guides, and devas. These are forces or entities that exist to help people during their lifetime. This makes it possible for you to trust life and allow it to guide you. I call this way of living the "allowing lifestyle." You're allowing the life-forces to guide your life. When you face a problem, you trust the life-forces to provide you with solutions. In some Asian religions, they call this process "going with the flow."

You may have experienced this in your life. When you were at a crossroads, you may suddenly get a feeling about which path to take. Or, when you were stuck with a problem, someone came out of the blue to give you a hand. If you have, you were experiencing the allowing lifestyle. The following is an example.

> *I'm in Guam to design a highly classified system. I had received no information on what I was working on. I sat there with a stack of classified documents, wading through pieces of information.*
>
> *Jack, one of the Guam engineers, stopped by my desk and asked how I was doing. I told him not very well. He chuckled and told me to stop. He went back to his desk and returned with a magazine. On the cover was a drawing of what I was working on. Suddenly, the documents made sense.*

The allowing lifestyle is a different way of living. It can seem like miracles, as things simply appear or get done. It's important to know that allowing leads you toward your life's vision or purpose.

> *In some of my speeches, I've asked people to write their life's vision or purpose on the top of their handout sheets. As I walked up and down the aisle, I glanced over to see what they had written. In most cases, the sheets were blank. The attendees didn't know where they wished to direct their lives.*

If you haven't consciously picked a vision or purpose, you'll continue doing the same thing, day after day. The life-forces will guide you to maintain your present situation. You'll be living in your comfort zone, going nowhere in particular. However, this doesn't mean you're trapped. You can simply pick a purpose and go with it. I suggest you write your purpose down and paste it where you see it every morning. This makes it clear to the life-forces where you wish to go. When the change is radical, it takes trust to just head off in a different direction.

Allowing Led My Life

I recently looked back at my life and realized that I was always being led. I seemed to have had the mindset of allowing, except I was oblivious to it. As I reflected on all the critical points in my life, I saw how things and events were supporting me. They revealed the right path I needed to take. I thought it was the same for everyone.

> *At my grandmother's funeral, my uncle convinced my parents to have me train in Aikido. That led me to practice meditation every day. When you start before the age of seven and do it your whole life, you eventually become an expert.*

> *As a senior in high school, a friend asked me if any mainland colleges had accepted me. When I said no, he asked if the University of Hawaii had accepted me. My*

blank look prompted him to ask if I had applied. When I asked if I had to, he showed me how and I got accepted.

During the last semester of my senior year in college, one of the engineering students asked me if I had a job lined up. Again, I had done nothing. He said there were a few engineering recruiters on campus that day and asked me to join him. I did and got a job that started the day after graduation. This happened over and over.

When they eliminated my position due to lack of funding, one of the other engineers led me to get another job. I started working the week following my termination. When I wanted to move to Arizona, I got a job with almost no effort.

When I later wanted to move to Washington State, obstacle after obstacle came out of the blue to stop me. If I had moved, I may not have gotten a divorce. The financial debt from the divorce led me to seriously pursue my spiritual development. It then guided me to quit my job and withdraw my retirement money. I started a publishing company, published my dream book, and became an author. Those career changes allowed me to meet and marry my wonderful wife. That allowed us to start a speakers bureau. It also allowed me to become a full-time public speaker. Without that sequence of events, I would probably not be here writing this book.

I think an explanation is needed here. I wasn't stupid or unaware. I was extremely shy and rarely spoke to anyone. As a student, I had two friends in my neighborhood. We only got together to watch movies at the nearby theaters. We never discussed school or anything else. It seemed natural that things always went my way, regardless of where I was or what I was doing.

Take a moment to look at your life right now. Have you noticed how unseen forces seem to lead your life? Did certain solutions or choices you made seem like miracles? Have you felt lucky or thought that a guardian was watching over you? If you have, you're aware of the allowing lifestyle.

Allowing for Two

As I mentioned above, I wanted to speak and help people. The following will illustrate how the life-forces work when you allow them.

My wife Andrea and I knew nothing about the speaking business. In the late 1980s, we didn't even know there were professional speakers. We offered seminars and created a book mail-order company. These did not do well.

One day, a Tucson news anchor needed help and called Andrea. He had a guest coming on his show and his guest wanted other media exposure. He asked my wife if she would arrange that and drive his guest around. She agreed.

The guest showed up, and we drove her to the television studio. His guest was Dottie Walters, the owner of a speakers bureau. As we drove her to her other engagements, she kept talking about professional speakers and starting a speakers bureau.

Arriving early at the airport, she asked what we did. She said I should be a professional speaker. She told Andrea to start a speakers bureau.

Two weeks later, a speaker who was also a consultant showed up to speak to a corporate client in

Tucson. He called to ask if we had some time; he would give us some advice on the speaking business. The flood gates opened as speakers called and offered more advice.

With all that, you would think we should have been successful. But having no experience in the speaking industry, we were steadily draining our remaining funds. Finally, we discussed paying the consultant for a consultation. It was expensive, but we felt we had no other choice. He told us what to do over two meetings. We manually put together a 6,000-piece mailing and took it to the post office two weeks before Christmas. After completing that, we needed a break.

We got inexpensive flights to Hawaii and spent Christmas with my folks. When we got back, Andrea looked at our checkbook. We had just enough to pay our next mortgage. If this didn't work, we would have to get an actual job.

Andrea said a prayer on New Year's Day. On the next working day, the phone started ringing. We were booking speakers! We've been successful for over 30 years.

Can you see how the allowing lifestyle worked out for us? It was a lot of work. It took a couple of years for it to pay off. But in the end, it was and still is an exciting and worthwhile adventure. The question to you is, can you use the allowing lifestyle in your life?

Not Allowing

Occasionally, I failed to follow the allowing lifestyle. Back then, I let my ego and thinking get in the way.

In the late 1960s, my good friend Glenn said he was going to an investment presentation. It was presented by two well-known mutual fund companies. One was Vanguard and I believe the other was T. Rowe Price. The funds sounded good, but their high fees made me think I could do better on my own. I invested in some stocks and was lucky to break even. My friend invested with one or both funds and did very well.

Payback

Sometimes, you do things that just don't make any sense. But then, it felt like the right thing to do. Even when it turned out to be wrong, I believe it was necessary!

I had a friend while living in Hawaii. I can no longer recall his name, but I remember he was a nice person. His life had always been difficult, and he seemed to be getting nowhere. When I was leaving Hawaii, the government would pay for only one car to be shipped to California. We were planning to buy a new car in Arizona, so I gave our other car to him. I was leaving in a couple of days, so signed the ownership papers. He promised to have the title transferred to him.

A year later, I received a letter from the State of Hawaii. They found my car abandoned, and I needed to take care of it. So, I flew to Hawaii, paid several fines, and had the car towed to the junkyard. I tried to call my friend, but his number was no longer in service. Having to get back to work, I returned to Arizona.

What happened? I later saw this as a lesson of being too trusting of people. Even now, when someone promises to do something, I believe they'd follow through. It was my nature to trust people. This was my wake-up call. Even now, I still think I'm too trusting of people.

If you have a negative experience, it may have been necessary. You may never know why it had to happen. But you should know that for some unknown reason, Dharma found it necessary for you to have your experience.

Is Life Predestined?

When people asked me if life was predestined, I always thought it was. After all, that was my experience and how I lived my life. I was always being led to do the right things at the right time. For me, life was doing my best wherever I was. I would always be open to the next thing to come into my life. Here's how I started in metaphysics.

> *I attended a metaphysical session and saw my high school teacher in the front row. I said, "Hi Bill, I bet you don't remember me." He turned around and his eyes drifted above me. He began telling me where I worked and what I had been doing. It impressed me that he knew more about my life than my parents. He then took me under his wing as a mentor.*

Similarly, I was walking to my publishing company's office when I saw my future wife.

> *She was sitting in the hallway, waiting to be interviewed. It stopped me because she had this glowing light around her. I knew only special people in my life exhibited that when we first meet. She turned down our position and got a job with another publisher.*

> *My company, along with her company, started the Tucson Book Publishing Association. At the monthly meetings, we kept having the most interesting conversations.*

> *At the National Booksellers Association Convention in Los Angeles, I'm standing at the bus stop. When the*

*bus doors open, Andrea steps off the bus in front of me.
The next day, I walked out of the Anaheim Convention
Center. I stopped and didn't know where I was going. I
turned around and, to my surprise, Andrea walked out
of that same door. We started chatting and had lunch
together, away from the maddening crowd. I thought
this was how it was for everyone.*

As you can see, my life appeared to be predestined. When you
realize this is happening to you, you may also believe that your
life is predestined.

The bottom line is simple: your life is not predestined. You
have free will. You can change your life at any time. However,
your choices may or may not be the best ones for you. Look at
your life. Are you enjoying your life? Is it meaningful and
fulfilling? If not, perhaps you need to consider the allowing
lifestyle or make a change using your free will.

People Fear the Allowing Lifestyle

Most people don't believe in living the allowing lifestyle.
They probably think it's only acceptable for ancient or backward
societies. In today's fast-moving, take-charge lifestyle, the
concept of allowing seems so foreign. You're taught how you
must be the master of your fate. If you make the right choices,
you win; make bad choices and you lose. It took me a while
before I finally understood the modern complexity of life and the
interplay of karma, life-forces, allowing, and free will.

A word of caution: There are a lot of con artists coming with
all kinds of wonderful-sounding offers. Be careful. In today's
communication media, it's so inexpensive to contact people. Be
wary of email, social media, and robocalls. They have such clever
ways to entice money out of people. Whenever you receive a
too-good-to-be-true offer, it's probably a scam. This is an
opportunity to learn what you should not do to others.

My Purpose

Why was it different for me? Why wasn't I repeating my yesterday's, as in Yogi Berra's déjà vu all over again? Looking deep into my life once more, I had one repeating dream from a very young age. I would always ride up on a white horse to rescue someone riding a black horse. These dreams sound so elementary and corny, but they were my dreams. The person in trouble was usually my cousin, Peter. From a dream analysis standpoint, I wanted to help people and I wanted to do it powerfully, as represented by the horse. It was this mission or purpose that was driving my allowing lifestyle.

What's your mission or purpose in life? When you choose it, the life-forces will support you. They'll gently guide you in the right direction. It's like having the GPS on your smartphone. When you decide where you wish to go, you'll be guided to your destination. If you make a wrong turn, it will either direct you back to your previous route or choose an alternative pathway. You can negate this with free will and choose to go in a different direction.

When you're heading in the wrong direction, the life-forces can redirect your life. When I spent more time and energy off my path, the life-forces would stop me. They wanted me back onto the "helping people pathway."

> *This occurred when I first surfed the larger waves on the North Shore of Oahu, Hawaii. I was coming down the face of a large wave when a surfboard came flying out of the whitewater. The board smashed into the side of my face. That force was such a jolt that I unconsciously grabbed my board as I fell. I knew better, but it was too late! I was stuck against my board as I rolled in the white water. With all my strength, I could not push that board away from me. Suddenly, the board snapped away from me and I was free. I swam to shore*

and picked up my board. I sat on the shore and contemplated what had just happened.

That was the day I stopped riding big waves. My swollen face and the blood flowing freely from the teeth cuts inside my mouth made me realize I could get killed out there. I eventually lost 2 teeth and had one tooth capped. It was time to get fully back into metaphysics. I stored my surfboard under my parent's home and my dad used my surfboard as a storage shelf. I also sold my scuba equipment, golf clubs, and gave up deep-sea fishing. I was getting back into my allowing lifestyle.

Rather Die than Speak

Speaking was one area I wanted to avoid at all costs. The idea of reading something in class scared me. I was not only afraid of answering a question in class; I even hated answering the telephone. Just thinking about giving a speech had sweat, not perspiration, pouring out of my body. My fear made it impossible for me to share a joke or story with two of my friends. However, the forces of life had other plans for me.

When I got to college, Speech 100 was a required course in Hawaii. That year, "Y as in Yamamoto" was the last to register. After securing my other courses, I couldn't fit the few remaining Speech 100 openings into my schedule. So, I skipped it. The same thing happened when I registered for the second semester. I thought it was great and simply forgot about taking my speech course until my junior year.

My counselor reminded me I had to have Speech 100 if I wanted to graduate. When I tried to register for Speech 100, I couldn't because it was only open to freshmen. They assigned me a similar speech course with one difference; I had to pass a review board of three speech instructors other than my own or take another speech course. For the next four semesters, I kept passing different speech courses and failing the boards. In my last semester as a senior, I begged the board to pass me. I told them I was graduating and had a job waiting. My instructor spoke with the board members and may have told them I had a hearing impairment. When the board approved my release, I swore I would never give another speech as long as I lived.

Before the end of my first year at work, my boss tasked me to teach design classes to new engineers. My metaphysical teacher also asked me to teach a class on dream interpretation. I asked her why I needed to teach any class. She said sharing personal growth information was the reason I came into this world. It was the first time someone said I had a mission. I worked on my speaking ability and put in countless hours of teaching. In time, that allowed me to become a full-time professional speaker.

I now realize how my allowing lifestyle guided my need to speak to people. The life-forces made certain things happen automatically, guiding me to where I needed to be. My karma also helped me, as you'll see in the next chapter. If you have a feeling that you're being directed in a certain direction, you're most likely correct.

Guides and Helpers

You also have guides or helpers who are there when you need them. In the east, they call these devas or divine beings who help you. While some may consider devas to be evil, I find them supportive. You also have the support of angels and archangels who are a part of western religions. They represent similar divine forces with different names.

Religious people have also asked for assistance and help from saints. They pray to complete difficult tasks or gain healing for family members, friends, and themselves. This group can also include family members who have passed away. They are all a part of the life-forces providing you with guidance and advice.

Non-believers may call it luck or just the odds favoring them. But you know better! During quiet moments, you may have sensed their presence. You may have had contact with them as a part of a dream experience or as a vision during meditation. You may have caught a movement in the corner of your eye that verified their presence. It's best to avoid all forms of recreational drugs. Drugs dull your senses and prevent you from receiving guidance from your life-forces. To understand another powerful and driving force in your life, it's time to understand the forces of karma.

Summary

When you wake up tomorrow morning, don't rush out of bed. Instead, lie there for a moment. Consider the idea that life-forces were working on you during the night. And today, they'll help you achieve what you desire. However, you need to reaffirm your purpose to let them know where you're going. They'll begin their subtle efforts to guide and help you. You'll need to be aware to see the direction you're headed, evaluate that it's safe, then trust and do it.

Are you the change you wish to see in the world?

Code 5: Karma & Long-Tale

Are other people the problem, or is it me?

You are a child of the Source. Your body is the same stuff as the all-powerful Source that created the entire universe. When you realize this, you probably feel you should have been born a perfect example of a human being. After all, if you were the all-powerful being, the Big Kahuna, you'd want to have perfect children. As Number One, you would also want to have beautiful children who were intelligent, compassionate, healthy, and happy. Every child would be powerful so they can continue to create wonderful things in this ever-expanding universe.

Yet, as you observe how people behave, you know this can't possibly be true. People are not born physically perfect. They can do foolish and even stupid things. Everyone can have repeated moments of anger, hate, and fear. They can have extended periods of suffering from frustration, worry, and sorrow. A few can become so unhappy that they want to end their lives. And you can guess that no one gets up in the morning and says to themselves,

"Hey, this looks like a great day to screw up the rest of my life!"

And yet they do! And they do it over and over! Then, they get upset and try to blame something or someone else for their problems, including their spouse or significant other. They may also blame inflation, business cutback, and the down economy! Others may pick a more acceptable scapegoat, such as a bad and uncaring boss.

So, what's the real problem? What's keeping you from making your life your way? How is it that your life often sucks when you thought you were doing well? And sometimes, even your best efforts end as failures. To explain life, religions often say that life is unknowable. Science says their theories don't fully explain human behavior. They attribute irrational human behavior to defective DNA, irrational thinking, emotional madness, and/or mental illness.

Creating Karma

You may be familiar with karma. It's often called the Law of Cause and Effect. In the West, it's referred to as "What goes around, comes around." Your past seems to influence your present life. But karma is not the idea of payback that most people believe.

Back in the mid-1970s, my mentor told me that karma was nothing more than "emotional memories stuck in time". You probably just had the same thought I did.

"What?"

How does an emotional memory stuck in time have anything to do with karma and my life right now? That idea bugged me. As usual, I stored that information because I knew it would someday be important.

Karma is the continuous process of recording everything you do in your life. It's not just your good or bad deeds that get recorded, but everything you ever said and did. It's like having a multi-dimensional movie of your whole life with every thought and emotion included. That process never stops as you continuously add more memories.

Your Long-Tale

An instant after you create your karma, it gets stored. It joins all your past life memories back to the beginning of creation. I call this storehouse your "long-tale". This is not a typo. Your long-tale is your complete memory history of everything that has happened in this life and all your past lives. It's your long story.

You carry your long-tale with you. Every cell in your body has a copy of your DNA and your long-tale. This allows your cells to do their job. Each cell knows how to reproduce itself perfectly until aging, abuse, and pathogens prevent it from doing its job.

Activating Your Long-Tale

Whenever you do anything right now, your actions activate similar memories stored in your long-tale. If your actions are good and in line with improving your life, your long-tale memories will support that. Your long-tale places similar memories in your brain. You now know more and learn faster with the added memories. You'll be able to overcome present limitations and more easily rise to another level. If your actions are negative or terrible, your long-tale will also support that. It can show you how to excel at being bad.

Your long-tale can have a huge amount of knowledge and skills from all your past lives. When you're learning to play the piano, having music in your long-tale will accelerate your learning. If a child has grandmaster memories in their long tale, that child may progress so rapidly and may be considered a child prodigy. This occurs in fields that were practiced in the child's past lives, such as sports, math, art, music, and languages. These children brought out the wonderful talent and abilities they had learned in their past lives.

You may have unique talents and abilities stored in your long-tale. If you're interested in art and have higher math memories in your long-tale, those memories can help you make rapid progress in computer art or computer games. It may not make you a child prodigy or a gifted artist, but it will help you excel.

Perhaps your long-tale contains memories of being a talented cook, a mighty martial artist, or an exceptional athlete. These memories can make it easier for you to learn and progress quickly in those fields. You'll know you have the help of your long-tale when the topic is easy, and you make rapid progress.

Successful People

When you look at successful people, you could see them as having lots of good karma. Their long-tale is supporting whatever they're doing. They add to their long-tale support by doing more in their field of choice. That adds more expert karma to their long-tale. Their thoughts and focus add additional long-tale support to their present efforts. If they encounter a problem, they work hard and turn it into an advantage.

Earlier, we discussed how these people continue to expand what they're doing. If they're in business, they're expanding their products and services. If they operate a charity, they're doing more of it.

While a person may have good karma in business, they may have bad karma in their relationships and/or their health. You want to be sure that your new karma (daily activities and thoughts) is in line with all the important areas of your life.

People Who Suffer

When you find a person who's poor or homeless, you can see them as having bad karma. They seem to be trapped to remain where they are. To change their lives, they must stop complaining about what's wrong. They need to think positive thoughts and follow through with positive actions. This will bring in a fresh line of support from their long-tale. That will start improving their lives.

Unfortunately, many will stubbornly choose to remain where they are. When people offer to help, they turn it down. When people suggest possibilities, they say it's not an option. They may have lots of reasons and excuses why they can't improve. They may believe that they only deserve to remain where they are.

When people are continuously pushed or insulted, they may push back. When pushed hard or over a long period, that person may push back even harder. In a few cases, they may take a weapon and retaliate. These people need to handle their stress. The best stress management methods are found in my book, *Stress Management is Easy.*

Addiction

There are many types of addiction. The ones that receive the most attention are based on destructive behavior and results. These include alcohol, smoking, and recreational and prescription drugs. On a lesser level, you can add overeating and sex into this category.

I'm going to discuss this by using a fictitious person I'll call Alpha. Many of Alpha's ancestors were addicted to alcohol. After all, alcoholic drinks were the drinks of choice when drinking water was dangerous. Alpha's DNA may also influence him to be inclined to become an alcoholic.

Alpha's long-tale has stored emotional memories of being an alcoholic in many of his past lives. These long-tale memories will remain dormant until Alpha has a drink. When Alpha takes his first drink, his long-tale activates a memory of drinking. Alpha's memories may be of enjoying himself and having a good time while taking a drink.

If Alpha only has one or two drinks socially, it will trigger his social drinking tendency in his long-tale. He will seek opportunities to go out and have a fun time, having a drink or two. This is enjoyable and not a problem.

But suppose something terrible happens to Alpha. Suppose his significant other leaves him or he loses his job and can't find another. If Alpha uses alcohol to escape his stress and/or fear, a new set of emotional memories gets triggered. When he gets wasted, his long-tale alcoholic memories get activated and will support his behavior. He won't know this consciously, but the emotional memories will help him to keep drinking. Depending on the individual, it may just take one heavy drinking bout to trigger Alpha's emotional memories that will unconsciously push for more.

This happens with all the addictions we mentioned above. The only way out is to go cold-turkey and never start again. My dad quit a multi-pack smoking habit in his early 20s. He only stopped when his doctor told him if he didn't stop, he would be dead in a year or two. He stopped and lived to be 98 years old. In the same way, Alpha must never trigger the addiction again. Once triggered, it will be a long and difficult battle, fighting his long-tale emotional memories that are pushing for more.

Creating Your Life

Life can be tough. You now know you had a lot of things working for and against you, such as:

- Your DNA from your parents and their ancestors.
- Your long-tale memories.
- Your emotional state.

You understand how your DNA and long-tale memories affect your life. Here we introduce another concept—your emotional state. Your emotional state influences what you perceive through your five senses. The stronger your emotional state, the more it alters what you experience.

If you're angry, you'll view your life and experiences through angry lens. Your negative emotional state will activate long-tale memories of being angry. They will further amplify your anger. If you have a lot of long-tale anger memories, people may see you as having a short temper. When you get angry, you're altering what you perceive. You then react through your anger. You've lost control over the situation and your emotions have taken over. Other negative emotions include frustration, hate, and fear.

If you wish to have a happy life, you need to find ways to be happy. If visiting a friend, taking a walk in the park, or going to a movie makes you happy, do it. When you do, your long-tale will bring more similar memories to your brain. Life will be happier for you. Other positive emotions include love, joy, and peace of mind.

To prosper and enjoy life, you need to create prosperity and enjoyment in your life. If you desire to be wealthy, have the thoughts and feeling that you're wealthy. Then be sure you have the knowledge and skills to excel in your area of choice. If you wish to have peace of mind, look for ways to create that sense in your life. Whatever you desire, create that in your life and your long-tale will support your choice.

> *When you change how you look at things, the things you look at change.* — Max Planck, theoretical physicist

JEDI Knight

> *I learned this wonderful idea from my friend Willie Whitefeather. I had just arrived to share my two children's books with an elementary school class. As I approached the room, the children were chanting, "JEDI Knight... JEDI Knight..."*

A couple of minutes later, Willie came out of the room. After a quick bear hug, I asked him about the JEDI Knight thing.

Looking astonished, he asked, "You don't know about Star Wars and the JEDI Knights?"

"Of course, I do. But why did you have the children chanting JEDI Knight?"

"Jedi is an acronym for 'Just Everyday, Do It!'"

Wow, what a great way to remember to repeat a positive exercise. I believe I asked him for permission to use that story. But if I didn't, I'm just borrowing it. Sadly, Willie is no longer with us.

Summary

Karma is everything you think, say, do, and feel. This is the "cause" in your life. All of it gets stored in your long-tale. When you do anything that your long-tale memories can support, it sends these supportive memories to your brain. This becomes the "effect" in your life.

The primary key is your need to maintain positive thoughts, words, actions, and feelings. These are the triggers that release positive memories and abilities stored in your long-tale. Whatever you choose to do, feel confident and do the best you can. Your long-tale will support you.

When you do good, life is good; when you do bad,
life sucks!

Code 6: Clearing Karma

Create good karma or you may not like the results.

When your life sucks, who's always around? Yep, it's you! But then, you're always around when life is wonderful. This means you're a part of the cause of whatever's happening. With karma in your life, whatever you're doing is being supported and multiplied by your long-tale. Do something stupid and you'll get more support to do something stupider. Go out and get drunk and your long-tale will support you to keep you there. Steal something from a store and you'll want to do more of it more often. If you want your life to improve, you need to stop doing stupid things. You can then follow it with the intelligent or smart things you want in your life.

No matter what's happening, it never helps you to get upset and retaliate. That instantly creates new negative karma. Other negative memories emerge out of your long-tale to make your life worse. Instead of reacting, leave and find a nice, quiet environment. This is where your ability to meditate comes in handy. You'll benefit by being a silent observer of what's happening.

Up and Down for No Reason

Sometimes, you may suddenly feel depressed or angry. You don't know why you're feeling this way. I've found it often results from a subliminal trigger from an old, negative memory. The trigger may have been something you just happened to see or hear. Perhaps it was someone who passed you in the supermarket that vaguely reminds you of a person who cheated you long ago. Or you may glance at a magazine headline that activated the feelings of being depressed from your long-tail. You're being blindsided by your long-tale and you're not aware of it.

Leaping Long-Tale

You'll recognize the long-tale activation when you're feeling okay, then bam, you're not! You can't find any logical reason why you just got hit by the emotional change. It could be negative, making you feel afraid, frustrated, angry, or even depressed. Or it could just as well be a positive feeling that your life is wonderful, you're happy, and you're ready to go out and take on the world.

If you got hit by a downer, then you need to work on it. To stop feeling down, change your thoughts and actions. Think of something positive, such as admiring the plants in your yard or enjoying the scenery. You can do something positive, such as calling a friend or relative you haven't spoken to in a while. If nothing else comes to mind, have a small snack of your favorite treat. This will improve how you feel.

Another solution is to meditate and maintain a silent mind. Without thoughts, these negative moments and feelings will pass. You can also take on the attitude of "and this too shall end." Just realize that nothing is forever.

There are also times when you suddenly feel energized or happy. You don't know why, but you feel ready to take on a new project or improve your diet. Again, it's probably another subliminal memory that triggered a wonderful memory. When this happens, just smile and enjoy the moment. Then do something positive which will bring on more wonderful memories from your long-tale.

Forgive

I'm a realist. I know you may have the strongest intention of living a positive life. But sometimes you may react strongly and even violently. When someone repeatedly interferes with what you're doing, you can scream or threaten them. This is happening around the world, in gross and subtle ways.

If this ever happens to you, try to remove yourself from the situation. If you must resort to force, do it with a silent mind. When it's over, start forgiving the other party. It doesn't matter who did what to whom, just start by forgiving people. Forgiving others minimizes the emotions attached to this event's karma. It's best to forgive others silently. If you say it out loud, they probably won't understand. You can then forgive yourself.

Don't join the mass of humanity seeking revenge, as in taking an eye for an eye. Western religion seems to have forgotten that they are to "give an eye for an eye," because vengeance belongs to the Source. Those who forgive others, get it! They realize there's more to life than what meets the eye.

Intention

Sometimes, life isn't that simple. Your intent has a powerful influence on your karma. What was the reason for your action? Did you hurt or even kill another to stop them from hurting or killing others? If saving other people was your intent, then it results in positive karma. This is especially true for police officers who may have to hurt or kill to protect themselves or the innocent. The same is true for soldiers who must kill others in the line of duty. It's best not to harbor any anger or hate for others to minimize negative karma.

The Source knows the true intent of every action. Regardless of what the world sees and how it reacts and judges, you and the Source know the truth.

Be Kind

As you interact with people, you could start by being kind. No, you don't have to be a pushover. Nor do you have to understand or support them. But could you just be kind and considerate? They are also struggling with their long-tale. Most probably don't have a clue about karma and their long-tale; they are just struggling in the dark.

Let's say that a family member married someone you don't like. You don't know why, but you don't want to associate with that person. As a result, you've been treating them coldly and saying nothing nice about them. After all, they're not your type of people. You may feel you're above them or they seem so snotty. While you don't think there's anything wrong with your behavior, you've been adding negative karma. It may have already come back to bite you, or it'll happen soon.

When someone has had little or no past life relationship with a family or group, that person may have a difficult time fitting in. You gain a lot of points by being kind and treating them fairly. They may be a new family member, a relative, a work associate, or even a neighbor. Realize that you and they are both struggling with different long-tales and theirs could be a large and heavy one. Just treat people kindly!

Summary

By doing good, you empower your life. If a problem occurs, forgive the other party, and remember to forgive yourself. However, when you suddenly feel down for no apparent reason, mindfulness and meditation are wonderful solutions. Also, have a positive intention behind your actions and be kind to people. Never put others down to raise yourself; that action will go against you.

Doing good prevents the negative rising from your long-tale.

Code 7: Illusions & the Metaverse

You've been experiencing the world through warped and colored lenses.

Life is an illusion. Yeah, I know you've probably heard that from some guru or read it in some spiritual book. They teach how everything in your life is an illusion and not real. Everything you see and touch is not what's there. Whatever you smell or taste is not the actual aroma or flavor your nose and tongue experienced. You've never had an authentic experience!

Your natural response to the above statements is probably, "That's either stupid or crazy?" After all, you seem to have authentic experiences. When you bump your head, it's real, and it hurts. You may have attempted to run through a cement block wall as Harry Potter did, only to find that wall was painfully solid and unyielding. So, who or what is creating the illusion?

The Illusion Creator

The creator of the illusion is you. You do it automatically all day long. There is almost no time when you aren't creating illusions about every experience you have. You're better at creating illusions than the best magicians in Las Vegas.

At this moment, your eyes, ears, nose, tongue, and body are sending electrical impulses to your brain. The amount of information entering your brain is tremendous. For instance, your eyes transmit the entire picture of what you see, even the tiny details you aren't even noticing. It's sending a completely new picture from each eye, at almost 30 times a second.

While this barrage of inputs comes flooding in, your brain is working to categorize and record the information. It takes the input from both eyes and converts them into a three-dimensional movie. It's also analyzing, rendering judgment, and adding your personal feelings to what it sees. What you perceive may or may not be what your senses sent to your brain.

As an example, suppose you're observing a scene at the beach. Your five senses send information to your brain about what they observe. Your conclusion is simple: This is the most beautiful and relaxing beach you've ever seen.

You're shedding clothing and walking towards the turquoise water. A local person is describing the beach on the phone. You stop and listen in,

"Hey man, this beach is the pits. The sand looks dirty, and I see cups and food paper plates lying all over. I hear the druggies hang out here at night and they found needles lying in the sand. And you won't believe the stink from the bathhouse. Try to eat with that smell and you'll puke. We'll meet at another beach, a mile north of here!"

Who's right? Well, you both are. Your brain saw and drew its conclusion about what you experienced. When it overheard the local's description, your brain used that new input to consider and even override your previous opinion. After all, the local person should be a better and higher authority on local beaches.

So, which one is the truth? Neither one! Can you see how all your experiences are illusions created in your brain? One person may love eating sturgeon caviar, while another finds it repulsive. A few Icelanders may love the flavor and aroma of fermented shark meat, while others can't escape the smell fast enough.

There are only relative opinions based on your experiences and beliefs.

Creating Illusions

If someone says you should eat eel sushi, you may look forward to having a novel experience or automatically hate it.

> *This happened at a sushi restaurant with my father-in-law. I pointed to a piece and told him he had to have it. I mentioned it'll be the best-tasting sushi he'll ever have. He gingerly picked it up with his awkward chopsticks and asked what it was. As he brought the sushi up to his mouth, I said, "It's eel." The sushi stopped a couple of inches in front of his mouth and floated back down onto the plate.*

> *In his mind, he heard the word "eel" and probably thought of "snake." It immediately stopped him. The thought of eating a piece of snake meat was something he could never do.*

In the same way, your brain takes everything you experience and modifies it. You've been creating illusions for so long that you're not aware that you're continually doing it. You color every experience with your emotions, needs, beliefs, fears, hate, prejudices, likes, loves, and desires. You continually miss out on what's really happening.

Filling Bins

To simplify your brain's continuous need to process incoming data, it creates storage bins. Each bin holds a specific, common experience. When your brain receives any input from your five senses, it automatically tries to fit that experience into an existing bin. When it locates a close-enough match, your brain sticks that experience into that bin. It doesn't evaluate the input or render judgment about it. Your experience is what your brain has previously concluded about that bin.

Suppose you happen to see a political campaign poster. You have a bin for republican politicians and democratic politicians. When you know a politician's political party, you stick that person into the appropriate bin. You don't care what the person believes in or stands for. If she's in that party, she must be like the rest of them.

On the other hand, suppose you love everything, Tesla. You have an "I love Tesla" bin and that's it! There is nothing that will convince you otherwise. If someone asks what you thought of the new Tesla models, you'd probably unconsciously reply,

"Yeah, great cars, love them, nothing's better!"

Your answer came without a thought. It simply took the normal answer from the Tesla bin. You know what you know, and you don't want to be confused with new information and facts.

Bins Are Efficient

Your brain uses bins because it can't observe, listen, feel, taste, and smell the dozens of continuous inputs every second. It has no time to completely observe, recognize, listen, understand, evaluate, and draw a conclusion on all these inputs on a split-second basis. If you had to process every single input, you'll be on input overload in a very short time. Instead, your brain sticks most inputs into appropriate bins. Once there, your brain can use your previous evaluation and opinion, if it's ever called to do so.

Your mind has bins for all your common and unique or memorable experiences. You have bins for your thoughts and feelings on clothing, colors, and music. You have food bins with automatic responses to bacon, sea urchin, pizza, 100-year-old fermented eggs, macaroni and cheese, and escargots in garlic butter. And your bin conclusions may not agree with the bin conclusions other people have. Whenever you have a completely new experience, you'll create a new bin for it. If you're with someone you respect, you may take their opinion and/or evaluation and change your bin's conclusion.

So, if a health practitioner says that eating green bitter melon is good for you, you might try it at a Chinese restaurant. Or you may already have an "I hate bitter foods" bin. Then, bitter melon is close enough to fit into that bin. Without thinking, you'll turn down eating a bitter melon dish, even when others are saying how unique and tasty it is.

Bin Overload

When you're very busy or there are too many things going on, your brain struggles to dump inputs into bins. If there are no similar bins, it struggles to process those inputs. As the information continues pouring in, your brain can't handle it all. It overlooks a lot of the inputs it's receiving. You can see that this causes miscommunications and misunderstandings. When this happens, you're suffering from input overload. If this continues over a long period, you'll suffer from mental burnout.

As speaker bureau owners, we regularly attended the annual National Speakers Association conventions. Throughout the day, there were multiple speakers giving sessions on different topics, such as marketing, product sales, the use of social media, and presentation skills.

Speaking with newer speakers, some have reached information overload. The amount of information being presented, along with personal experiences during breaks, has overwhelmed them. A few would retreat to their hotel rooms to digest what they've learned. I've heard of a few who left the convention, having taken in as much as they could handle.

Meanwhile, the veterans with more than a decade of speaking experience were sitting in the back talking with friends. When asked, they say they've heard it all before. They have their neat little bins holding similar information on every aspect of the speaking business.

Then there are a few veteran speakers who are sitting in the front row of every presentation. They are taking notes, listening for any new angle or how to put a new twist on an idea that would help their business. They may not be getting new information but find an effective presentation style or skill.

Bins make processing information more efficient and effective. However, it can prevent you from getting the subtle new angle of a topic you already know. It takes discipline to pay close attention to capture the subtle differences each speaker provides.

Removing the Illusion

Meditation also allows you to remove illusions. When your mind is silent, there are no thoughts, opinions, judgments, or anything else being created. The data continues coming in from your senses. You're just observing what's happening. You see things and events for what they are. This gives you tremendous clarity.

The strength of karma is in the emotions attached to a memory. When your mind is silent and there are no emotions attached to what's happening. These won't activate emotional memories from your past. You won't get upset or overreact to what's happening. With silence, you won't experience work overload or mental burnout. You're not taxing your brain with thoughts, opinions, fears, judgments, prejudices, and desires. Instead, all your observations are treated calmly and given fair treatment.

Being silent doesn't mean that you're permanently living without thoughts. You must think to read the newspaper or the terms in a contract. You're also thinking to write notes and instructions. You'll evaluate everything with thought based on its merits and demerits and then take appropriate action.

While silently observing, be aware of what's happening inside of you. You may get signals on what to do or not do. You may receive signals on which direction to take or what decision to make. You may also receive intuitive flashes that clarify the situation you're facing.

A Simple Illusion

Stop and observe people for a minute. You can see how your mind comes to almost instant conclusions. You see someone and your mind gives you information about the person. It may say the person is good-looking but appears to be a little slick. Somehow, you don't feel comfortable, and you can't trust that person.

Professional speakers should know how quickly they're evaluated when speaking to an audience. The emcee introduces the speaker, who then walks onto the stage. Tests have shown that most of the attendees know if they'll like or dislike the speaker's presentation after hearing a few words. Some may have drawn their conclusions as the speaker walks up to the center stage. They'll then listen to the speaker's presentation only to confirm their initial evaluation. If attendees have a negative sense about the speaker, that speaker has a long uphill battle to change their minds.

Suppose you're having breakfast at a restaurant with friends. The person at the next table leaves and everyone simultaneously notices a $100 bill left for the server. Your friends comment on what they saw:

- "She's showing off how rich she is."

- "Maybe she made a mistake?"
- "She's an idiot!"
- "She probably had nothing smaller."
- "I'd do that if I had her money."

If you maintained a silent mind, what would you see? You'd see a person who was generously leaving a tip. That's it! The conclusions from the others at the table were from their own experiences, needs, jealousy, and fears.

Living in the Metaverse

Another way to look at the world of illusion is to see it as living in your personal metaverse. Everything you see is a simple line drawing. As the creator of your metaverse, you have a pallet of paints to color everything, including yourself. These paints are different feelings, thoughts, beliefs, energy, and judgments. You're the master of this metaverse. You can change everything and everyone to represent whatever you desire.

Stop and look at your metaverse at work. Is it positive or negative? Who are the people you like and the ones you wish weren't there? You know who will support you and the ones who'll probably throw you under the bus. You may have the same situation at home.

But you must remember that you're the creator of your metaverse. You're the holder and user of the paintbrushes. You control which color you place on each person and item you have. If the overall artwork you created sucks, you have only two options. You can repaint the people and your environment or go somewhere else.

You're the grand master of your metaverse. You built this world based on your beliefs. You own the excitement or dullness of your experiences. This is your moment to build a new future in your metaverse. As you transform your life, possibilities appear before you. You have two choices. The first is to stubbornly hang on to what you've created. The other is to change the painting you have of yourself and the world around you. If you choose the latter, hang on and ride the possibilities which promise to be different.

Summary

Life is an intricate network of illusions. When you see the world as your metaverse, you can create or re-create it in any way you wish. Start by transforming yourself and you will automatically change the world around you. Some of you may change the world for the benefit of all.

Nothing has any real intrinsic value other than
what you decide to assign to it

Living the Source Code

Using the source to maximize your life.

You're now ready to apply the Source Codes to get the most out of your life. You can use these as a guide on how to live your life. Some of the Source Codes, like Karma, may be familiar to you. But now you know they exist and what they can do to and for you. The Source Code is life's cheat sheet to transform your life and make it the life of your dreams.

Source

Your essence is who you really are. This is the source that allows your physical body to do things. When the essence leaves the body, you're no longer alive. But this essence, the real you, can't die! Physical bodies may come and go, but the essence continues. Knowing your essence can't die should give you courage.

This doesn't mean you should become fearless and do reckless things. Life on Earth is a privilege and an opportunity. You may have to stand in line to get another lifetime here. So, use this knowledge to gain the courage to do what's right. But not to where you do stupid things.

And remember that love is the force that maintains the universe and our world. Live a life filled with love. And this doesn't mean you should have sex with as many people as possible. If you leave a bad or negative karmic scar, it will be there in your long-tale to haunt you.

Prime Directives

Discover what's possible: There's no mention of what you need to do. It's saying don't keep doing things the same way.

Whatever you're doing, work on doing it differently. Do something creative or different. If you're always quiet, talk a lot, or tell a story you find interesting. Otherwise, today is like yesterday's story and it will become tomorrow's story. You could wear something different at work.

When I first started working a few decades ago, all the engineers wore dress shirts. We had "Aloha Friday" in Hawaii, and the engineers wore aloha shirts. That was so boring, so I did the opposite. I wore aloha shirts every day and put on a dress shirt on Friday. That became too much of an anti-social thing and made me stand out. Being shy, I kicked wearing dress shirts on Fridays and stuck to aloha shirts. As the dress code relaxed, we all began wearing polo shirts to work.

Enjoy life: People say it's hard not to enjoy life living in Hawaii. But living in Tucson, Arizona, I also found life enjoyable. Meanwhile, I also realize that life was tough for many people. I would meet some of them while teaching classes in the evenings. As I listened to their stories, their lives were like reading a novel of pain and suffering. I knew I could not directly change most of their lives. Doing some research, I found they were reliving their karmic past from their long-tale.

Learn from mistakes: When you're suffering, you need to change your life. Of course, you may do what most people do—they asked, "How?" The "how" is their lesson. They are to discover their own "how" and begin transforming their lives. You may start a side business and fail. That's okay. You have the opportunity to learn why you failed. You can then start another business and not repeat the same mistake. It's the same story for a failed marriage. Learn from your mistakes and make sure you don't repeat them.

Dharma

Dharma makes sure there's order in the universe. It makes it possible for you to be born again to live another lifetime. Even if you're the worst screw-up in the history of the world, you're coming back to try again. As you evolve to a higher level of living, it's even possible to go on to different countries, other systems, and even dimensions. In Dharma's world, you should know there are always consequences, as in rewards and limitations.

Your purpose determines the direction of your life. Dharma and the life-forces will assist and guide you to achieve your purpose. Be sure to record your purpose on paper. Read it each morning to help to guide you in the right direction. You can also change your purpose or vision as many times as you need or desire.

Karma and Your Long-Tale

Karma is whatever you're doing right now. It records your thoughts, words, and actions. It includes your intent, emotional state, and any subliminal desires. All this gets stored in your long-tale.

What you do right now triggers support from your long-tale. If you don't like the results, you need to do something different. You need to simply look at your thoughts and actions. These generate the support coming from your long-tale. You need to do different things, or at least do them differently. If you bump your head every time you enter this room, you need to bend over so you don't hit your head. Or you can enter another room.

My mentor, Bill, was a high school principal. Every year, a few of his students would come to him and say, "I don't know how, but I'm pregnant." He would then run to the window and look to the left and right. A bit shocked, they asked him,

"What are you looking for?"

"The last time this happened, three wise men came."

You may chuckle, but everything you do has an effect. Your today is being driven by all your yesterdays. But what you're doing right now has the most powerful effect. If you want your life to be different, start doing different things. You always get back what you give to the world.

The bottom line is simple. You get what you give out. Do good and you get good. Do bad and your life sucks!

Allowing

You need to get your life in order. You need to realize that the Source has your back. If you die, it will give you another chance. There will always be another chance until the end of time, whenever that may be. This is the law, even if you don't think certain people deserve another chance.

You're living the prime directives. You should discover possibilities and find ways to enjoy your life. You also learn from mistakes and try to never repeat them. When you make a mistake, you forgive everyone. Then remember to forgive yourself.

You do good and know you're supported by your long-tale. It also has your back, as long as your actions are for the good of all concerned. I put this in because some believe as long as it's good for them, they don't care about anyone else.

The life-forces also have your back. They will try to contact you, but you need to be aware and listen to hear their messages. They may control events, so you have a better chance to succeed. Their actions are always trying to help you, even if you disagree with the results.

While you are always being led by your life-forces, you also have free will. You can always choose another path, other than the one you're now on.

There will always be forks on the road. When you reach one, you need to decide which one to take. You can logically process the most feasible option, or you can allow life to flow. Allowing is to trust the life-forces to guide you to make the right decision. As always, the choice is yours.

You may also decide to wait and think about it, but you can't wait forever. No decision is the decision to stand at a fork in the road and do nothing. When you don't know what to do, you can take Yogi Berra's advice and just take one of the forks. With no decision, you're wasting your time and missing out on the next adventure in your life.

A word of caution here. If the choice appears to be a problem or dangerous, take a moment and consider the consequences. Does it make sense to do this? You'll recall that when I wanted to publish my dream analysis book, I did what most people would never do. I could have waited 10 years for my full retirement and then try to publish my book. Instead, I quit my government job, withdrew my retirement money, and started a publishing business. I didn't know about publishing, had very little funds, and Jeff Bezos would not start Amazon for another 10 years. But it somehow felt as if the life-forces were with me, and I allowed it to happen.

Illusion

You're the mighty creator of how you perceive your life experiences. Your mind can make your life a wonderful or miserable existence. You make your life miserable if you hate your job, your boss, the commute, your home, and/or your neighbors. Your life would improve if you could at least love your home. Then you couple that with liking your job, even if you can't like your boss.

But then, you are the creator of your life. You can change it all because it's all being created in your brain. There's nothing that says your boss is always seen as terrible or bad. Other people may like him or his management style. Some may even love him. So let me repeat this: you are the creator who makes your life wonderful or miserable with your choices.

Using the toys that are being called the metaverse adds another illusion on top of your illusions. This is neither good nor bad—it's just different. Fortunately, meditation allows you to see life clearly. It removes the emotional and mental coloring that your brain and the metaverse added.

Or you can take control of your perception. You can see life your way. You can enjoy your life more, regardless of the situations and circumstances that surround you.

A Polynesian Allowing Lifestyle

I found many people living a relaxed allowing lifestyle in Polynesia. Many of them have lived painful and traumatic past lives. They have chosen this slower lifestyle to rest and recuperate. A lot of these people are living in tropical climates or small communities. For them, life is to take it easy and enjoy. I met such a man while working in Hawaii.

He was a cab driver on the military base where I worked in Hawaii. I was curious about his background and asked where he was from. He said he was from Samoa and was a Samoan Chief. He kind of looked the part, being a handsome and tanned person with a large frame.

I wanted to know more about him and asked what his life was like living in Samoa. He said he would just take it easy and have fun. In the morning, he would send his sons out to go fishing in the ocean. He would send his daughters to harvest the fruits and vegetables from their gardens. What they brought back would be their meal for the day.

I asked if he sold any of the extra fish or fruits. He said no; they only took enough for the day. Tomorrow, his children would go out and do it again. There was always enough for everyone.

Having had such a relaxed lifestyle, I asked him what he was doing working here in Hawaii. He said his children were now getting married and having children. With a larger family, he needed some money to buy more land. As soon as he had enough, he would go back home to Samoa. His last words were, "It will be soon." He'll be returning to his family for more rest and recreation.

The Chief and his family are living the allowing lifestyle. It's easy enough to criticize people who seem to love doing little to nothing. In our hustle or fear of being left behind in society, they appear to be slackers. Some people in the Americas live the "mañana" or "I'll get to it in the future" lifestyle. In Hawaii and the South Pacific, they often call it "Polynesian Paralysis."

Summary

The only person you can successfully change is you. By changing how you view yourself and the life you live, you are on your way to transforming your life. While transformation seems simple, most people find it difficult and either quickly give up or never start.

In my upcoming book titled *Change is Easy*, I've reduced change into a process. While the process is simple and easy to understand, the execution may prove to be more difficult.

When the world appears to change, you've changed.

Simplify Your Life

Our life is frittered away by detail. Simplify,
simplify. — Henry David Thoreau

Simplifying your life may not be a simple process. You've
spent your entire life finding and accumulating everything
you have. When you acquired these, they were useful,
important, expensive, and/or meaningful. But today, much of it
has lost its original purpose or usefulness. Now, they may simply
occupy a part of your physical space and a part of your mind.

Take a quick survey of what you have. You'll realize how
many things you have that you haven't used in years. You'll find
items you'll never use again, such as outdated equipment or old
tools. These not only clutter your home and workspace, but they
also clutter your mind.

When you look at each item, consider what purpose they
serve in your life today. You'll find that most of your holdings
serve no real purpose anymore. Instead, they impede your
physical life while taking up mind units you need to think and
process information.

When you walk through your home, you'll subconsciously
remember when you got each item, what it cost, what it was for,
and how you were going to use it. When you pass unfinished
tasks, they'll wonder when you'll get back to them and take up
additional mind units. At what point do you shift from being a
collector to becoming a hoarder? Only you can make that
decision when to begin seriously simplifying your life.

A friend's brother in New York just passed away. His
apartment was small but filled with things. He had
stacks of papers, broken equipment, and junk-filled

boxes from floor to ceiling. There was only a narrow pathway to walk through the apartment. Only one of the three bedrooms had a place to sleep. When my friend went to help clean out the apartment, he was afraid to touch anything for fear it would cave in and bury him under the trash. He told his brother's daughters it would be best to hire professionals for their safety.

Taking Action

Pick one room or piece of furniture to start your cleaning process. If you wish to start with an entire room, the following are the common rooms where you can start:

- Kitchen: especially the items in the refrigerator and freezer.
- Garage: items held in closets or tool chests.
- Closets: don't shift items from one closet to another.
- Bedrooms: under the bed and in the dressers.

The first thing you need to do is commit yourself to taking one of three actions. These are to keep, trash, or hold. That's it! There are no other categories that you'll consider. You'll do this because there are a lot of items you'll put into your "hold" category. There is a catch in placing an item on hold. In less than a week, if you aren't going to keep them and assign a designated place to store them, you must trash them. I know of people who have kept a hold pile on the floor for months and even years. That's the sign of a "hoarder" in the making.

Starting Somewhere

You'll pick a room or a piece of furniture to start. It's best if you start small. Let's say you picked a dresser. You'll begin by emptying everything in the drawers and placing them on the floor. When you do this, you may realize just how much stuff you've collected. You may find items that have duplicates, things you've never used, and items that you no longer need.

You'll need three pieces of cardboard and write on them: KEEP, TRASH, and HOLD. Start by placing items into three groups designated keep, trash, and hold.

Keep Items

Take everything in the keep pile and put them back where they belong. If you did this right, you should have a lot more space in your dresser. It should look more organized and even beautiful.

Trash Items

At noon on the sixth day, the contents in the trash pile are given away to charity or placed in the trash container. One word of caution. Things are difficult to give away. Your best bet is to give it to a charitable organization. You may take it down to a local group or picked up from a national organization, such as:

- Goodwill
- Green Drop
- Salvation Army
- Big Brother Big Sister Foundation
- Vietnam Veterans of America
- Habitat for Humanity
- AMVETS

If you wish to donate in your neighborhood, consider that this will take time and effort. If you decide to place it on the Internet or a neighborhood site, you need to take photos and then create a description. Then, people may or may not show up to pick it up. My relative tried to give away beautiful Koa furniture in Hawaii. The only person who wanted it lived on the other side of the island. They even asked if my relative would deliver the furniture to them. Your best bet is to donate your large trash items to an organization that picks up your donations.

Hold Items

You'll maintain your hold pile for six days. During that time, you'll go through what's there and keep only what's useful or precious. By noon of the sixth day, you'll stop and commit everything in that pile to the trash. That's it. No turning back. You will trash or donate everything. You must avoid reasons and excuses why you can't get to trash the items on hold. Once you do that, it could be a month or more before you get back to trashing that pile.

If you're living with someone, there may be serious discussions on unique items. You must refrain from arguing, which creates bad karma. This is especially true about sentimental items, such as gifts from parents or awards and recognition. These will keep your mind focused on the past and not on the present or what we refer to as the "now." More about this in the next chapter. But for now, it's on to the next piece of furniture or room.

Organizing

When you organize your furniture or room, you need to assign a place for everything you've kept. When you use an item, you'll return it to where it belongs. You must also require others to do the same. This will save you from looking for things the next time you need the item. Things will always be there, exactly where you placed them. It will simplify your life.

Summary

You may find that simplifying is not simple if you're living with someone else. What you may consider junk or clutter may be precious and meaningful to them. You need to be patient when asking others in your life to simplify their clutter.

Simplifying is also difficult because it's not a one-and-done process. You'll continue to buy more things and receive gifts. Your needs will also change. Once a year, review your home to consider if you need to simplify it. You'll love the freedom and time saving you'll gain.

Meditation

Silence opens possibilities.

Meditation is a straightforward process. All you need to do is maintain a silent mind for a little while. It sounds easy enough. After all, your brain is one of the few things you should have total control over. So, sitting and having no thoughts for the next 15 minutes should be simple. Or is it? Are you one of those who has tried to meditate and found it to be very difficult or impossible?

You need to practice meditation because it offers you a lot of physical, emotional, and mental benefits. It provides many health benefits, as found in my book, Meditation Is Easy. You may also receive insights or guidance while meditating. Be especially careful when dealing with money and safety. You shouldn't practice meditation while driving a car or operating machinery. Your tendency may be to relax and shut your eyes. That could create a dangerous situation.

Let's be honest here, for most people, meditation is difficult. Even monks and others who have practiced it for 30 or more years couldn't maintain a silent mind. I found it to be difficult until you can do it. But once you get it, you'll wonder why it was so difficult. Fortunately, I began practicing meditation before my 7th birthday. Even then, it took me over 20 years before I could meditate and maintain a silent mind.

Why is Meditation Difficult

Most people find meditation to be difficult because they believe thinking is the most important aspect of life. Most people believe René Descartes' idea that they exist because they think. People subconsciously believe that by thinking, they exist as human beings. Their ability to think places them above all other forms of life. The underlying message says if they stop thinking, they have no way of showing their supremacy. In fact, without thinking, they can't prove they even exist. Without their thoughts, they don't feel alive as human beings.

And along comes a long list of gurus and saints who have been saying that thinking does not empower you. They believe that thinking causes all of your problems. They claim that when you stop thinking, you'll gain new insights into life. You'll release yourself from a self-imposed prison to gain freedom. According to them, your goal is to achieve a silent mind and then become enlightened. Enlightenment frees you from having to return to Earth for another lifetime.

The Methods

We're going to simplify this process. There are thousands of books on meditation. They will essentially teach you similar methods, giving a few specific details. So, we'll use the simplest and fastest method possible.

First, no special clothing or accessories are necessary. Just dress comfortably. Sit comfortably. This means that you shouldn't try to sit in a full or half lotus position unless you can do it without any pain. Your hands do not have to be on your knees with your thumb touching your index finger. Nor do you have to hold your hands below your belly button, on top of each other. Just be comfortable and sit upright. A straight back allows the energy in your body to flow smoothly.

Mantra Meditation

The most common method is mantra meditation. This method requires you to chant a sound. That's it! You may choose any sound or use one that your instructor or guru gave you. The sounds that have been used for thousands of years are the "om" and the "aum."

Sit for about 15 minutes and chant either of these or your own mantra. You'll do this with no expectation of a result. You're simply sitting and chanting. While you're doing this, be aware of what's happening to you or your body. You aren't expecting anything, but you're aware if anything occurs. If this is difficult, you may decide to join a group of common-minded meditators.

Led Meditation

Another common meditation method is "led meditation." Here, an instructor or recording tells you to sit comfortably and close your eyes. You'll hear the music coming from a recording. You'll close your eyes and use your imagination to follow his instructions.

> *A common scenario has you walking up a hill. At some point, you'll come to a large open field that has a beautiful view of the mountains. A large waterfall is coming off the side of the mountain. There's a mist from the waterfall reflecting the sun's rays in a rainbow. You'll sit by a stream and listen to the calming sound of water passing over rocks. You'll be told to feel the different colors of the rainbow that are reflecting its light onto your body. You'll sit there enjoying the sound of the tumbling stream. The music continues as you're told to go deeper within.*

There are benefits to using this form of meditation. Unfortunately, most people are not attentive. As they listen to the recording, they tend to fall asleep. I've known many people who use led meditations to fall asleep. You need to sit up and be aware to gain the benefits of meditating.

Zen Meditation

Zen Buddhism teaches a slightly different method of meditation. The instructor or monk will tell you, "You're just sitting. You're not trying to have a vision or insight. You're not trying to be enlightened. Don't expect anything. You're just sitting and being attentive."

You'll then follow their suggestion and sit with your eyes closed. You'll try to be attentive. If you nod or doze, they'll tap your back with a stick to keep you attentive. Some schools believe a hard rap with a stick is a better reminder to remain alert.

The key to meditation is to have a silent mind and be aware. You're aware, but not aware of anything in particular. Awareness is being attentive without being focused on something. You're just sitting, your mind is silent, and you're awake and aware.

You're Silent

One day, bam, you open your eyes and realize you were silent and aware. You've done it! Is it time to celebrate? Are you now enlightened? Are you ready to be a guru and teach others how to meditate?

Sadly, the answer is no. Having a silent mind is just the beginning. While having a silent mind gives you a lot of benefits, enlightenment is not one of them. Silence allows you to see more clearly. Your mind is not jumping in with your beliefs, prejudices, fears, and desires. It's not judging, condemning, or praising anything or anyone you met or saw. You won't be worrying about bills to pay, deadlines to meet, or things you forgot or need to do. It's just seeing things for what they are. You'll have a powerful ability to focus your attention on one thing.

Silence also gives you peace of mind. When you get upset, stop, and observe how your mind is chattering about why you're angry. It continues this barrage because when it stops, you can't be upset. You become calm and peaceful. Politicians and the media don't want audiences who are silent and calm. They want you to be agitated, supporting a cause, or upset about what's not happening. They want you to vote for them or tune in and raise their ratings.

Silence also allows joy and love into your life. Being silent gives you peace of mind. Gaining love, joy, and peace of mind in your life is definitely worth the effort of achieving a silent mind. We'll cover that in another book.

Beyond Silence

When you achieve silent meditation, you've only begun to see what meditation provides. Being silent brings you so many gifts. These include creativity, innovation, implicit understanding, knowing, flowing, allowing, and so much more. Experience life in silence will grow until you'll live most of your life with a silent mind. I know this because I've been able to maintain a silent mind for nearly 50 years. To get there, I learned and practiced many forms of meditation. But I mostly just sat every day until I realized I was not thinking or projecting images. It took me a long time before I realized I wasn't thinking. My mind has been mostly silent for nearly 50 years.

But Wait, There's More

Not thinking is just the beginning. You'll also be able to maintain a silent mind while walking. When you're at work, you'll find your job is probably a series of repetitive tasks. While doing those, you'll be able to maintain a silent mind. You'll find it wonderful to work and play with a silent mind. Nothing bothers you while your mind is silent. I wasn't bothered when my SUV was pushed off Interstate 10 between Phoenix and Tucson.

> *My wife and I were driving on the highway at 75 mph. I maintained my "cool" when an 18-wheeler suddenly changed lanes and pushed our SUV off the road and onto the rough median. Heading towards the cement barrier, I pulled the car back onto the highway. I barely missed the back end of the 18-wheeler and the SUV spun out into two or three 360-degree spins on the highway. We're not sure how many spins because it was at night. I only saw a series of headlight flashes, followed by darkness. My wife and I remained calm, and she said a silent prayer. A few seconds later, we stopped. My wife saw another 18-wheeler that was about to hit us broadside. She yelled to "gun it" and I did. It barely missed us as it flew by the back of our vehicle.*
>
> *Verifying we were both alright, I got back on the highway. There were a lot of vehicles stopped on the road behind us. They must have witnessed what had happened. The culprit 18-wheeler and the one that barely missed us were far down the road.*

This is a benefit of having a silent mind. Of course, you may be one of those who believe that it's dangerous to drive without thoughts. You don't understand what silent living is like until you've done it for a while. As I mentioned before, I've spent more than half of my life with a silent mind. Thoughts are only required to read and write, such as I'm doing right now as I'm writing this book. I'm not doing what others have called automatic or channeled writing.

In time, as you go deeper into the silence, there's so much more. In silence, you're tapping into the nature of life. If you are interested in going deeper, I recommend you get books about the lives and experiences of saints, mystics, and gurus who have gone there. It will open your mind to more of what's possible.

Summary

Commit to sitting somewhere safe and close your eyes. You're just sitting and aware of being here. You have no expectations of what may result. Just regular silent sitting already has its rewards. It helps you both physically and psychologically. To get more information on meditation and the mechanics of group meditation, consider reading my book *Meditation is Easy.*

Lessons Learned

Purposeful living creates a life worth living.

One of the key roles you have is to learn from your experiences. This is not like learning in a classroom. You won't be reading and discussing how you should handle potential problems in your life. Instead, your learning will come from your daily living, as it's happening in real-time. This means that when a problem or situation occurs in your life, that becomes your classroom. It's the perfect setting and scenario for you to learn!

Simplify the Process

There are all kinds of situations and problems you'll encounter throughout your life. You'll have happy moments and painful situations. Sometimes tragedy enters your life through no fault of your own. At other times, you may have caused the problem. Whenever you have a problem, it's an opportunity for you to learn from the experience and about life. It will be an in-your-face, live experience. And there are no limits to how many of these you will experience in a day, week, or lifetime.

When a situation occurs, become a silent observer. This doesn't mean you're going to stop and watch what's happening. Instead, you'll be an aware and active observer. If you're involved, you'll take appropriate action. Your only difference is having a silent mind. Yep, you read that right. You'll remain silent while taking part in working or solving what's happening.

In time, you'll be able to maintain a silent mind while discussing what's happening. You won't engage your thoughts, even as you share ideas or give suggestions. Being silent will not allow thoughts, and you won't become emotionally upset, frustrated, or angry. You can do this!

How do I know? I've lived this way most of the time. During long driving trips, I can discuss things while having no thoughts. I've discussed ideas at work without any thoughts. I have given many 90-minute presentations to corporations, trade associations, and government agencies without a single thought. The words just come out of my mouth. In fact, there were a few times when I said something I never knew or said before. I almost wanted to stop and say to the client, "I want to take a few seconds to write this down. This is great, and I've never thought or said this before."

Any great speaker is not speaking out of memory. She knows her material so well that she can probably give it in her sleep. However, while she's giving her presentation, she's observing the audience. Are the attendees getting my message? Should I include another example to clarify the point? Am I speaking too fast that the people are not getting what I'm saying?

Listening to Myself

In my case, it began in the middle of a speech. I became aware that my mouth was talking, and I was listening. I wasn't thinking about what I was going to say. I became an observer of my presentation. It was fascinating. I heard the words at the same time the audience heard them. I only glanced at the computer to know I was on topic.

I know it sounds freaky, but it can be done. I know I'm getting a bit off track here, but you need to realize that your thoughts are not the end all. Your words can come from your heart and best knowledge. When you've achieved a silent mind, you may do the same thing.

I later noticed how I often spoke without any thoughts. I would listen to people and my mouth would respond. Being attentive, I simply saw most interactions as an exchange of experiences, beliefs, regrets, and dreams. Going deeper would be difficult if ideas challenged the other party. For this reason, I've decided to write this and other self-development books to help people. Individuals should search and open themselves to new ideas on their own.

Learning

To learn about a situation or problem, you need to:

- Observe: Observe conversations and any action taking place.
- Contemplate: Sit to contemplate what occurred.
- Learn: What did you learn?

Observe

During any problem or confrontation, become the observer. This doesn't mean that you shouldn't protect yourself should the need arise. Nor does it mean that you don't take action to solve the problem. You'll do what's necessary while remaining silent.

Remember, it's most important to observe what's happening inside of you. You may want to criticize, argue, or even hit the other person. Or you may choose to step back and leave or even run away. Whatever action you take, do it with a silent mind. You're acting in your best interest and the interest of all concerned.

Contemplate

After the incident, take the time to be alone and contemplate the situation. You can start by asking yourself the following questions.

- What triggered the situation or problem?
- Was I a part of the cause or the solution?
- Did I get angry or emotional?

- Did I offend or injure anyone?

For now, you'll use your thoughts to ask and answer these questions. You'll see what part you played in the solution to the problem. If there was no solution, you'll understand how you handled yourself.

Learn

Here are a few questions you can ask to learn about yourself.

- What did I learn during my contemplation?
- If I was wrong, did I apologize?
- Even if I was right, did I still apologize?
- Did I then forgive the other party for their part?
- Did I also forgive myself?
- What will I do that's different the next time something similar happens?

Learning is a continuous process. Every day, there's something new to learn. It's one thing to learn from a television program or from reading a book. But your best lessons come from life. They are the real interactions between you and the world around you.

I had a plumber come a second time to fix one of our toilets. He was such a positive person, always smiling and seeming to be happy. I asked him what keeps him so positive and happy.

He said, "I always look forward to learning something new every day. Whenever I learn something new, it makes me feel good and I'm happy. And talking with you, I've learned and used what you've taught me."

We laughed, and I said, "And thanks for teaching me the third rule of plumbing: don't chew your fingernails."

It's so easy to say that we should stop polluting the planet and stop global warming. That's giving the power away to others and placing responsibility on them (whomever they may be). What's important is what you're doing about it. Are you minimizing trash, petroleum fuel, water usage, food waste, etc.?

Summary

Remember, you're here to discover possibilities and enjoy yourself. You'll also learn not to repeat mistakes. Keep transforming your life. If you can achieve this, then you're living a powerful and fulfilling life.

Are you living on purpose?

Love People

Love people! It opens you to a greater world.

Love is such a huge and powerful word. It's a powerful feeling, a bond you have with someone or something. It's a word you may have thrown around to signify the passion you have for another. You can love your significant other and the members of your family. It's just as easy to say you love a piece of art or a supportive friend. You may express a love of your country as well as love for your favorite football team. Along the way, love has become a gentler way of saying you want sex. You can toss around the word love to express your feelings towards just about anything. But the word goes way beyond that. It is so much more!

Speaking of Love

As a co-owner of a speakers bureau, we get to hear many stories about different speakers' great and terrible experiences. A fellow-speaking professional shared this story with me.

> She was a bit nervous as she waited to face the audience. These were young techies, mostly in their 20s and 30s. They all worked for a high-tech company you would recognize.

> The announcer introduced her, and her talk title included the word "love." Polite applause greeted her as she walked onto center stage. She began with enthusiasm on a topic she loved. With the bright lights shining into her eyes, she could barely see the audience.

> Five minutes into her talk, the people in the back rows began walking out. Soon she could make out a

steady stream heading towards the exits. Within 15 minutes, the auditorium was empty. Tears welled up in her eyes as she slowly walked off the stage.

Can you blame the audience? In their minds, love was their feelings toward science, technology, wealth, and sex. That was it. They couldn't see how that would help them at their jobs. Nor would it earn them a pay raise or give them a promotion. It was just another "woo-woo" topic from another "woo-woo" speaker.

Unfortunately, the speaker was just a bit ahead of her time. Today, the actual need of people is not to learn more about programming, sales, and marketing. Tech workers know how to do that. What they need is to find a way to mitigate the loneliness of working at home or in a cubicle. They need a shift of energy, as they often work late into the night and on weekends. They need a positive, face-to-face relationship with people and make a connection, a situation that Facetime or Zoom won't fulfill.

People find so many practical things to love. There's the love of money, stocks, and ownership of property. They can love their home, cars, possessions, and anything else they controlled. Then, there's also the love of family. Meanwhile, some treat people like trash and place their acquisitions on pedestals. Is it possible to do the opposite? Is it possible for your love to extend beyond you and your stuff?

What Is Love?

From a spiritual standpoint, love is the power or force that supports and maintains the universe. Stop for a moment and read that sentence again. It's the force that holds the universe together. It's the love that flows from the Source that empowers you. The Source gives you the energy to be a living action figure in the world. Without it, the universe ceases to exist, and everything goes back before the start of the present creation cycle. Love is the power that makes it possible for you to be you!

This is one of the great secrets of the spiritual world. Love is the great power that not only maintains the universe; it allows you to use that power. Of course, you must understand what it is and how to access it.

What Doesn't Work

We live in a world where pain and suffering are expected. People's lives are extended periods of worry, anger, and fear, sprinkled with brief moments of love and happiness. Politicians and elected officials create laws and regulations that frustrate the populace. People are angry when their lives are not improving and search for someone to blame. They hate anyone who they believe was the cause of their suffering.

You now know you should not have negative thoughts and actions. That will only activate your negative long-tale memories. They'll make your negative life worse. You need to create positive thoughts and activities in your life to get positive support from your long-tale. What's the most powerful force you can use to improve your life? It's love!

Where's the Love?

I've met a few people who've challenged me on the idea and power of love. When I say the entire universe is nothing but love, they ask why they don't feel it. I explain that it was there, but they are not open to receiving it. They have shut down their ability to feel love.

In Eastern theology, you have energy centers or chakras. One of them is near to your heart and is called the heart chakra. When it's open, it can send and receive love. But when it's closed, it's unable to sense or feel the power of love.

The heart chakra closes when a person suffers from the loss of a loved one. We have labeled this a "heartbreak." These people often close their heart chakra when a loved one or close family member dies. It occurs when a significant other leaves for another or cheats on their relationship. When the heart chakra closes, the world feels cold and uncaring. You'll sense little or no love from others, even those who are trying to help or comfort you. Your life closes itself off when it stops loving.

When a person survives with little love, they turn to negative sources of energy. These sources are frustration, anger, and hate. They may also be envious and jealous. Or their energy can come from worry and fear. You already know that this opens your long-tale to dump more of the same into your brain and life. A life empowered by negative emotional forces misses all the growth and transformation the person came into this world to experience.

Open to Love

The only way to open your heart chakra is to give love away. If you can't love another person, you can pick something safe. One method is to go out into your yard and send love to your tree. Admire the strength and beauty of the tree and send love to it. You can tell the tree how wonderful it is to have it in your life.

Or you can throw yourself into your hobby, something like painting or photography. If you're a photographer, play with different angles and lighting to get the best shot possible. Then, reviewing what you shot and loving what you've created. Love the entire experience of capturing this moment on your camera, and not just the final photo.

These actions will open your heart chakra. You'll know there's been a change when the world no longer appears so cold and distant. You may start to feel good about your life and where you are. You'll love and appreciate anyone who's in your life. Your long-tale will support this and make your life more loving.

Love also has the power to maintain your health and heal ailments. It gives significance to whatever you say and do in your life. It empowers your work and makes your life more enjoyable. It's the force that's the catalyst to transform and create the life you desire. Using the power of love successfully makes your life so much more meaningful.

Summary

Love people. You may also love things, but they aren't as important as loving people. When you love people, it opens your heart chakra to receive love. It also opens love in your long-tale. Love is the powerful force that binds the universe together. It's the force that helps and guides you to a more meaningful and fulfilling life. It also makes room for a life experiencing joy and peace of mind.

Love all fear not for we are one. — Satya Sai Baba

Receiving Guidance

Insights, guidance, solutions are always coming.
You catch them in silent awareness.

You are always in contact with the Source. This means there's a constant flow of communication between you and the Source. Unfortunately, you may miss the important messages if you're too busy or you don't believe it's of any importance. The following are a few of the ways you receive guidance.

Caution: In all cases, seriously consider if the guidance you receive sounds reasonable and safe. Be especially careful when dealing with money and safety.

Dreams

Your dreams guide you by answering questions and providing solutions to problems. If there's a significant event in your future, your dreams provide a psychic glimpse into that future event. With that information, you may be able to alter your future. You may often recall your dream guidance when taking a shower or later while driving a car. To extract the details of your symbolic dream messages, consider my dream books, *Creative Dream Analysis* and *The Power of Dreams*.

Intuition

You may receive intuitive flashes that come as a feeling in your stomach area. Some call it a "gut feeling." This feeling comes from the solar plexus energy center or Chakra. It provides you with a good or bad signal to let you know the probable results of what you're considering. Some people are more sensitive to these signals than others. When you receive one, it's usually best to consider following that signal rather than regretting not doing so later.

Insights

When approaching someone, you may get a sense of the person. You may tune into the person's personality or long-tale. Or you may see their emotional state in the colors of their aura (energy colors around a person). In all cases, insights are more accurate than what you've been told about a person. By listening to your insights and any intuitive feelings you have, you won't have regrets. You won't be saying,

"I knew I should have..." or "I shouldn't have..."

The dictionary of my book, *Creative Dream Analysis: A Guide to Self-Development,* lists the meaning of the different aura colors.

Meditation

You're meditating when your mind is silent. In time, you'll be able to speak and do things while having a silent mind. You'll see situations and people for what they are. Being silent is a shelter in today's environment, where you're bombarded by people, activities, media, and social media. These are all pushing you to believe or do something they want. You can get more information on this topic from my upcoming book, *Meditation is Easy.*

Contemplation

When considering hiring a person or trying to find a solution, contemplation is helpful. Begin by considering what's happening and what you desire. Then, silently wait for an insight or answer. The answer may come immediately, or it may take longer. Don't be impatient. There are always reasons for the delay, reasons you may never know or understand. The ideas that come from contemplation are not thoughts, but flashes of insight that come from another level of mind. Like your dreams, it may take a while to catch the insight.

Creativity and Innovation

Creativity is having an insight that goes beyond thinking to discover something new or unique. Innovation is having creative insights that solve a problem or situation. Both are your ability to find unique answers or solutions. You can understand more about how to get creative ideas and innovative solutions from your dreams in my book, *The Power of Dreams.*

Tapping the Source

You would think that this should be a natural ability of everyone on the planet. Well, it is! You have that ability right now! You can access that infinite knowledge at any moment. However, if you're not doing it regularly, you don't believe it's possible.

Many have called this storehouse of information the "Akasha," as found in the ancient Hindu books. The records are called the Akashic Records. Your long-tale is a tiny part of the akashic records. These records exist as a part of the Source, at a different level of existence.

All the experiences and lives of all life forms in the universe are stored here. It's so vast that it's beyond any brain's ability to fathom, much less comprehend. But you can tap the Akashic Records through meditation. You can ask your question and wait for an answer. If you can't get it that way, it may appear in your dreams. If it still can't get through, it may arrive in the future. If you ask and don't receive something immediately, don't give up. It may be hovering nearby, waiting for you to be silent to catch it.

Summary

You need to know that messages and directions may come at any time. It may come from a stranger or a relative. You may receive a feeling, a thought, or an idea while watching a movie. Avoid the tendency to negate an idea because it seems too far out. Instead, write it down. Smart ideas and solutions only appear to be stupid because they're different from what you know and practice. An excellent motto to follow is "never let a good thing stop something better."

Your Next Life

Astrologically, the world is moving out of the Piscean Age and into the Aquarian Age. I realize the expert astrologers will want to correct me, but the keyword of the Piscean Age was "belief". All religions and organizations were based on beliefs. You had to believe that the authorities or leaders knew what they were professing and claiming. The message of belief will not work in the Aquarian Age. This new age we're now entering is based on a different keyword, "knowledge". Individuals no longer simply believe the leaders and authorities. While they can go online and research answers, what they'll find will be based on the past. Instead, they want to know it for themselves through personal experiences or encounters.

What you've read previously in this book will help you gain your own experiences. I've used my life as an example of what you can do. But as always, my experience is not the holy grail of all truths. I expect that many of you will go further. You'll have a head start and will have greater and wider experiences than anything I've had. This book and its messages will guide you towards your own truths. May you meet your new insights and empowerment with humility and pass your experiences on to the next generation.

Onward

At some point in your life, it becomes time for your essence to abandon your physical body. Your body has served its purpose of providing you with a vehicle to experience life on this planet. It was not, unfortunately, designed or built to last forever. Science will try to extend your life, believing they can make it last forever. But there will come a time when the body is so damaged, it ceases to be of much use. Your essence will decide the right time to leave, and it will!

Many family members may try to keep your essence from leaving. They will cry or beg, trying to make you feel guilty for leaving them. But you will know when it's time for you to head off on your next adventure. You have lived your full life, and it is time to move on to the next. After leaving, you can decide what you should do. You may join the life-forces that are helping your family members. Or you can decide to move on to enter your next incarnation.

When you're ready to leave your body, you can do so with courage. You've been there countless times before, but you can make this one unique. You shouldn't be afraid or lonely knowing the life-forces will be there to guide you. To help you prepare, live your present life in a way that creates no regrets when the end comes. There's nothing left unsaid or unresolved. Forgive everyone and yourself for everything in your life. What you hold back will carry into your next life as a push to fulfill something you left undone.

The Physical

Your next life will be determined by a lot of factors you can't control. These include the environment that your parents have and will create. You also have no control over the DNA they brought together to create the foundation of your new physical body. However, there are things you can do right now to improve your future physical body and its mental/emotional capability.

Gain the knowledge that you can alter your DNA, by making certain genes turn on and others turn off. It's all dependent on your beliefs, your health (diet, exercise, and rest), and how open you are to possibilities.

The Emotional

Gain control over your emotions right now. Being angry is more than being stupid. It does you no good and ends up punishing your physical body. Anger also makes you coarse and less sensitive. Sensitivity is necessary to sense the flow of energy, gain insights, and receive guidance. Emotions out of control create tension and stress, which result in physical problems in your life.

Take steps right now to add loving and positive karmic memories to your long-tale. Although you have many millennia of memories in your long-tale, your latest memories will have a stronger influence. It will influence both this life and all your future lives.

The Mental

You can start by learning more about technology, health and fitness, finance and investing, maintaining a great relationship, and personal development. This knowledge will help you identify scammers and liars in so many areas of your life.

My work is guiding people to keep upgrading their personal development. I intend to use books and other information means to educate people. For me, it began with curiosity, became a passion, and is now what I consider to be my life's work.

The Spiritual

In the spiritual field, you can become more sensitive to the flow of your life. Look back at your life and see if you can recognize it happening to you. You may have called it luck, but it was there. Once you've verified it happened in your past, it's easier to live a more allowing lifestyle in your present life. But as always, you need to have a purpose and a vision of where you're going. It could be something as simple as being an excellent parent and raising a healthy family. Or it could also extend to being great at work or starting an entrepreneurial business. For those who are retired and healthy, you could help at the food bank to sort out donations or distribute boxes of food. That builds good karma and enhances your long-tale.

You'll carry the knowledge from this book and your life experiences in your long-tale. They will serve you well in your next life. When any of the topics are brought up, your life experiences from this life will enter your brain. You'll know a lot more than people expect. You'll know things you never really contemplated before and think it somehow just came flowing out of your mouth.

Fair Treatment

While it's said that the universe and our world are in balance, it certainly doesn't appear that way. There appears to be great wealth in the hands of a few, while poverty and great suffering for the masses. No matter how unfair life appears, everyone is being treated fairly by the Source. We are only reaping what we sowed. The people who are suffering are getting what they have done and are doing. There is no favoritism or imbalance in the Source's universe. We are all in this wonderful playground of life, bringing with us our talents and limitations. What you gave to the world and others is coming back, usually sooner than you think. Your present life reflects your past.

Meditation

Meditation is a key practice you need to work with. It is just sitting and having your mind become quiet. When your mind is silent, you become calm. A silent mind allows you to see things clearly. You simply see things for what they are. In time, you'll be able to work and play with a silent mind. You will use your thoughts when they are useful and beneficial. Otherwise, you'll be silent and enjoy life.

But meditation also takes something away from you. You lose your ability to be anxious and worry about what is happening or may happen in the future. When you're silent, you also lose the ability to become angry or to hate others. These states can't exist when your mind is not supporting these states. Also gone are jealousy and envy, which also need to be created and maintained in your mind. What you have left is peace of mind. The best part is—it's free!

For an older person, this is how to prepare for your next life. Remember, everything you do will either help or hinder you in the next life. I'm hoping this is your second-best life—with your next life being the best.

You Make a Difference

Every day, at any moment, you can make a difference in someone's life.

There are so many uncommon sources of wisdom found in the world. You may start by reading books. You should then graduate with practice and experience. The secrets of the universe await those with enough courage to take the journey. You have a choice: to either get up and go on the adventure or sit back in your comfort zone with your security blanket. The former is the spice and flavor of life; the latter is déjà vu all over again.

Every action you take can improve your life and the lives of others. Every word you utter can do the same. You don't know who's watching what you do or who's listening to what you say. It can either lift them up or push them down. This is an example from a fellow public speaker and friend.

Saving a Life

I stood in the registration line behind my friend I'll call "Bob" at a National Speakers Association Convention. Because it was a long wait, we began talking shop. I mentioned how great it was when someone comes to tell you how much you've helped them with a speech.

Bob shared how a man approached him as he packed his things at the end of a speech. The man shared his story of how Bob had saved his life. His life had gotten so bad that he was going to kill himself. He had straightened all his affairs and was sitting at his desk.

On top of the desk was the revolver he would use to end his life. On the corner of the desk, next to the revolver, he saw a note to the convention where Bob was speaking. He realized he could kill himself at any time. Since he had already signed up and paid for the convention, he would attend. Bob's speech so motivated him, that he returned home and turned his life around.

They were both crying as they continued hugging each other. Bob was crying because it was only a couple of years earlier that he had decided to end his life. He had a shotgun in his mouth and his toe on the trigger. At the last instant, he realized he was not supposed to do this, and stopped. The man helped Bob to understand the significance of not killing himself.

You Make a Difference

I shared this story with the members of the Arizona Chapter of the National Speakers Association and ended it with,

With every speech, you touch the lives of hundreds and even thousands of people. You may not know it, but there's always someone in the audience who's there to hear your message. You may not save a person's life, but you could make a significant difference in that person's future.

You may not know the results of what you say and do every day. A simple smile or an encouraging word may lift a person's outlook and improve that person's life. A nasty comment or ridicule may push a person down a deep and dark pathway from which he or she may never return. Be aware of what you say and do. You not only influence the lives of everyone around you; you're also creating your life.

Doing good is always enough.

Final Words

You create your world and the world responds.

Contained in this book is the synthesis of what I've learned from 70 years of meditation, more than 22 years of electrical engineering, over 40 years of teaching metaphysics, being a business owner and professional speaker, and serving as a priest. The contents of this book will work for you if you give it half a chance. After all, you are the child of the Source, a powerful and wonderful person. Regardless of what you've done in your life, there's always hope and possibilities.

The Source gave you everything you needed. Your present life is the sum of your gains and losses incurred from the beginning. What you do today will either be more of the same or the start of a new page in your life. As always, the choice is yours.

From your perspective, you're only here to experience three things. These are to discover what's possible, enjoy whatever you're doing or creating, and learn from your mistakes. You can take it easy to experience and learn a little. Or you can push to grow, expand, and learn a lot. It doesn't matter if you win or lose. Life is a long journey to experience possibilities, enjoy, and learn from your mistakes.

Every day comes with new challenges and opportunities. There are life-forces to help you through life. They are everywhere, trying to give you support and advice. To hear their messages, you need to be quiet; hence the need to meditate. To allow them to guide you, you need to be open-minded and get into the flow of your life.

Your life is the result of your karma. Every cell in your body holds the DNA from your parents, which they inherited from all your ancestors. Your DNA is most strongly influenced by your closest ancestors. At the same time, your long-tale awaits to assist you in what you are doing. Whatever you choose to do, your long-tale will help you if it holds supportive memories. You also have your free will to choose to do something different whenever you wish. Whatever you choose, your long-tale will support you.

Put this all together and you'll see how you are an illusion living a life of illusions. The following is a story of how Mother Teresa removed one illusion prisoners held about their lives.

Mother Teresa had just arrived in the United States. She went to a prison to speak to the worst criminals held there. She entered from the back of the room and slowly made her way to the front. The prisoners began taunting her.

One said, "Hey sista, what you gonna teach us that we don't already know? Hahaha..."

She quietly got to the front of the room and took out a large black marker. She drew a large circle on the whiteboard.

"This circle represents the whole of your life."

She then drew a little black dot in the middle of the circle.

"This dot represents the sin you've committed against humanity."

She then erased the black dot with the palm of her hand and said,

"And God forgives you for your sin."

Suddenly, she had their attention. Tears flowed out of a few prisoners' faces. She had touched them where no one else could reach. She made them aware that their whole life was not being a criminal. Yes, they may have committed one or more terrible crimes, but that was not their whole life. And their mistakes against society were easily forgiven by the only one who counted, the Source.

In the same manner, the whole of your life is not just one or two things. It's not just your work, regardless of how much you've accomplished. Nor is it any mistakes you've made or crimes you may have committed. It's not even about how famous you've gotten and all the media attention you've received. The whole of your life is a long and interesting journey through many lifetimes. You've done many good things and perhaps a few bad ones. But you now know that with each new lifetime, you get to start all over again.

You're not perfect. Neither am I. But you can begin transforming who you are and what you've done. You can start by improving your attitude and smiling more. Thank people and show you appreciate what they've done for you. You'll know you're changing when the world around you appears to change.

Right now, you are here to experience the wonderful possibilities that are available here on planet Earth. You are also here to experience all of life, from the painful and scary to the exciting and loving. When the world around you appear to be going crazy, you can silence your mind to regain your center and have peace of mind.

Each morning finds you waking up to the possibility of creating a whole new adventure. Your life only remains the same if you can't make even the smallest improvement. Life is about taking small steps every day. When you do this, you improve your life and, ultimately, your entire journey. You also open the possibility for a giant leap to occur. What you do today may appear to be tiny and insignificant. But it may also be the equivalent of a fluttering butterfly wing that became a powerful hurricane, improving life somewhere in the world.

About the Author

The best journeys in life are those that answer questions you never thought to ask. — Rich Ridgeway

Early in life, Gary realized he lived in a magical universe filled with unlimited possibilities. He spent his entire life discovering what's possible. He started the hard way, through books, teachers, seminars, and consultations. But the greatest lesson he learned was when he lived alone in the middle of the desert. Except for a minimum of time at work, he spent his time in meditation, prayer, and contemplation. The process lasted almost 9 months and gave him so many insights, experiences, and revelations. He also learned that most of his earlier efforts were unnecessary. What was important was the ability to silence his mind and live independently and sanely in a world of conflict and extremes! Yes, it's possible.

Background

Questions: Gary's grandmother passed away when he was almost seven. During the funeral, he heard the repeating question, "Why do people have to die?" It would prompt other questions, such as "who am I" and "why am I here?"

Aikido: His uncle, Sadao Yoshioka, convinced his parents to let him take Aikido. That caused him to meditate every day and master meditation. He had a major realization on energy as the demonstration attacker for the founder of Aikido, O'Sensei, Morihei Ueshiba.

Buddhism: While regularly attending Buddhist services for his grandmother, Gary wanted to become a Buddhist Priest. He studied Buddhism for a year until the Bishop of the Church said his Japanese was not good enough to learn and use Sanskrit.

College: Gary changed his life course and attended the University of Hawaii. He graduated with a degree in electrical engineering.

Engineering: For over 22 years, Gary worked as a civil servant for the US Navy and the US Army as an electrical engineer in communications and nuclear weapons.

Reiki: He was initiated by Hawayo Takata, at one of her first training sessions in Hawaii. Hawayo introduced the healing art of Reiki to the United States from Japan.

Metaphysics: His studies included reflexology, past life readings, meditation, group synergy, health and healing, channeling, massage, palmistry, energy transmission, dream interpretation, remote viewing, etc.

Teaching: His classes included dream interpretation, palmistry, personal development, spiritual development, and many other topics beginning in the mid-1970s.

College Instructor: He taught personal development and creativity classes at the University of Arizona and Pima College.

Priest: Archbishop Patriarch, Adrian Spruit, ordained Gary, a Catholic Priest in the Malabar Rites.

Publisher: Gary quit engineering and withdrew his retirement money. He founded Harbinger House, a trade book publishing company, which he sold in 1987.

Public Speaker: For 35 years, Gary offered presentations to corporations, trade associations, and government agencies.

Speakers Bureau: With his wife, he co-founded Gold Stars Speakers Bureau in 1989. It continues its successful operation at the time this book was written.

www.ingramcontent.com/pod-product-compliance
Lightning Source LLC
Chambersburg PA
CBHW071559040426
42452CB00008B/1225